THE SUBLIME HERITAGE OF MARTHA MOOD

MARTHA MOOD

THE SUBLIME HERITAGE OF MARTHA MOOD

LIMITED COMMEMORATIVE EDITION
Volume I

The story of Martha Mood,
her stitcheries,
and the tapestries woven from her stitchery designs.
Photographic illustrations by
Lester Kierstead Henderson.
Introduction and editing by Joseph Stacey.
Text by Lester Kierstead Henderson and Shirley Koploy.

KIERSTEAD PUBLICATIONS, Monterey, California

Printed in the United States of America
Published by Kierstead Publications, 712 Hawthorne Street, Monterey, California 93940

Library of Congress Catalog Card Number: 78-62391

International Standard Book Number:
Limited Commemorative Edition, 0-9601906-0-0
One Printing Only

Cover Illustration: Safari, horizontal stitchery.
Chapter Opening Illustrations: Martha Mood sketches for stitchery designs.

CONTENTS

PREFACE

While it has been in my mind to do the story of Martha Mood from the time of our earliest association, the real credit for this book belongs to Robert A. Weinstein, a historian with a deep sensitivity to art.

In the summer of 1974, I was scheduled for art shows in Victoria and Vancouver, B.C. To make this trip I joined a group of photographers on a cruise to Glacier Bay, Alaska. While en route on the *S.S. Arcadia*, I was persuaded to set up a show in the stateroom of Dr. Jack McGee of Sherman, Texas. Robert Weinstein, a man of whom I had heard but never met, attended the show. He was tremendously impressed. From his first contact with the art, he felt that he knew Martha deeply—her kindness, sensitivity, reserve, her brilliance and genius—without ever having met her.

Beginning at breakfast the following day, Robert insisted that I undertake a book on Martha. He would not let me relax until I promised that the book would be written and published. For the balance of the cruise, daily we discussed ways and means of getting this accomplished.

In September of 1974, I began the first of many coast-to-coast trips, photographing stitcheries, collecting information, and taping conversations with Martha's friends, her family, art collectors, and museum directors. This is the result.

This has been one of the most exciting and satisfying periods of my life, and I am most grateful to Robert Weinstein for having initiated it. Thank you, Robert, for your insight, knowledge, and friendship.

Lester F. Henderson

Martha Marie Mood Lehmann, June 21, 1908–July 15, 1972.

PROLOGUE

Martha Mood has been eulogized for her intellectual and aesthetic sensibility, her daring and complicated craftsmanship, her ability to blend concept and percept into works that are exquisite and magical. True, it's all true! But there are times when an individual forgets the artist completely—that wonderful moment when the "work is everything." Perhaps it is this mystical moment of viewer-object unity that is the ultimate tribute to an artist. And it is this type of moment I often find in viewing Martha Mood's stitchery. Undoubtedly her works are profound, distinctive, but those qualities are not the ones that I immediately feel. How many viewers will admit that their first reaction to a Mood stitchery was or is joy or better yet, euphoria. Whatever happened to Euphoria? What became of Joy? These are not titles for Gothic movies. They are questions answered by every Mood stitchery.

After all the luscious fabrics and rich threads were combined—and somehow all fabrics become luscious when Mood uses them, all threads become luxuriant when Mood works them—the Mood image appeared, a twentieth century visual counterpart to the poetry of the Man from Assisi who spoke with the birds and beasts!

Martha Mood advised would-be stitchers to develop "a seeing eye, an open mind, a little courage . . ." That advice is implicit in all her works, in all her designs, and it is essential to follow that advice in order to understand the genius of Martha Mood.

RUDY H. TURK
Director, Arizona State University,
University Art Collections, Tempe, Arizona

INTRODUCTION

by Joseph Stacey

Greatness in any field is ultimately measured by the length of time a given work maintains itself in the thought stream of a society, culture, or period. On initial exposure to the work of Martha Mood the viewer is immediately conscious of a touch of greatness that promises to endure the evaluation of history. The stunning impact of the reproductions depicting the consummate artistry of Martha Mood, American, confirms her standing as a woman of genius whose extraordinary measure of talents has elevated a handcraft to a fine art. With common materials, she achieved uncommon artistry.

The experience of enjoyment and appreciation communicated by art is a phenomenon defined as aesthetics, derived from the Greek word, *aistheta*, which means objects of sensuous as opposed to intellectual knowledge. This is the key to the enchanting mystique of Mood's creations. Here communication is achieved with art as the language. Make no mistake about it—art is another language, giving definition to feelings which otherwise might be formless and dumb. The language of Martha Mood's art is understood by museum curators and intellectuals, as well as by the average person.

The art of Martha Mood defies simple classification—it is at once folk art and fine art. It is American art; it is universal art.

Elise Jerram, in *The Sunday Peninsula Herald*, Peninsula Life Section, Monterey, California, July 13, 1975, wrote:

> *Flowers, children, nudes, dogs, cats, and animals of the field and forest were frequent Mood themes. She developed these subjects with stunning gradations and juxtapositions of color, and by richly varied textures.*
>
> *There is an element of folk art in some Martha Mood pieces, and of Byzantine opulence in others. Classicism pervades her ecclesiastical banners which hang in churches and chapels in the Southwest.*
>
> *The stitcheries are in a sense textile mosaics, composed as they are of bits and scraps of velvet and corduroy, satin and denim, gingham and lace—every kind of textured, printed and plain material imaginable.*
>
> *An essential element of her genius lay in her ability to take these disparate elements and recombine them into works of art.*

Academically, the definitions of "art" are many. For our purpose, we hold that art represents the human effort to imitate, supplement, alter or counteract the work of nature, creating a conscious arrangement of elements in a manner that affects the senses—generally produced by controlled ingenuity by one aware of his or her objective. The painter does it with palette and brush, the sculptor with matter and tools.

Writing in *House Beautiful* magazine in October, 1962, Martha Mood stated:

> *Stitchery has a unique and distinctive life and character of its own. There is nothing else quite like it. The potential of a sewn stitchery or an embroidered appliqué is as vast as art itself. The myriad qualities of countless fabrics, combined in myriad ways and enriched with thread and yarn, are a delight to contemplate. Its principal requirements are a seeing eye, an open mind, a little courage, and a craftsman's feel for the medium.*

But the above qualities alone could not account for Martha Mood's phenomenal creations. She had an inborn talent, what one associate called "a God-given spirit," that put her art on a level that most do not attain.

Wherever we find art it is the mirror of the period and a record of the people who produced it, reflecting their dress and customs and what they found to be important. For the most part, in creating art, artists have tried to make something they felt to be beautiful. When viewers too find beauty in the creations, they come closer to understanding the artists, as well as the state, region, country, or century in which they lived. In the broadest sense, art can be defined as the record of mankind's journey through history.

The importance, meaning, and eminence of an artist and his or her work grow in a measure proportionate to exposure, appeal, and patronage. Without national and international exposure and recognition, an artist and his or her work live only in the narrow confines of parochial and regional boundaries. Beyond those boundaries works of art expand and "come alive" as they are experienced and become part of the philosophical and psychological pattern of our cultural fabric.

The underlying purpose of this book is to put Martha Mood and her superb artistry "on stage" for the amazement and enlightenment of the critics, collectors, and authorities of the various "establishments" which influence the thought streams of art in America, as well as for the delight of the individual unsophisticated in the art field.

This is not only a graphic presentation of the quality and scope of Martha Mood's sublime heritage—it is also a revelation of the spiritual, moral, working and personal life of a wonderful, extraordinarily beautiful human being.

But for agent and co-author Lester Kierstead Henderson and a handful of private collectors, the existence of Martha Mood's art might have been only another fortuitous event in the cultural history of San Antonio, Texas.

Martha Mood is a genuine representative of American achievement. As an individual she had the inherent power to make and do rather than merely to exist and possess. Hers was a unique manifestation of creativeness. She realized that we develop and are

The artist holding one version of her "Ring-around-the-rosy" stitchery theme.

nourished by the strength, dash and color of our contacts and experiences with others. She became brilliant in the splendor of collectivity. San Antonio was the center of the world she loved. There, she was able to work and to glow, a bright star in the American galaxy. She interpreted the land and the people among whom she lived, accenting with knowledge and sympathy the primitive elements in the Western civilization she knew and loved.

The text of authors Lester Henderson and Shirley Koploy reveals an empathy, an understanding, an acutely intuitive insight into the person that was Martha Mood.

Martha Mood's early life was a rehearsal and prelude to the opera—with San Antonio the scene of the great and final act. She was successful in four careers and faced and defeated adversity several times against the odds. When bad luck was inevitable she accepted it, always thinking of the future—stepping out beyond the negative—making a polarity of good fortune and bad that resulted in her great art. She was not only in touch with her environment, she absorbed it. Her art was the sum of her life and in the end she herself was the masterpiece.

Those who knew her and treasure personal and intimate remembrances of Martha Mood share the tribute by one of her friends, the artist Winnie Noah:

The great thing about her was not her art, but her spirit, the person that she was. Without this she could not have produced what she did.

We who know her through the wondrous fantasies she created out of the simplest materials can neither ignore nor forget the spirit of Martha Mood and her unique art, for in it we see the spirit of America and we are inspired by it—a vital and eloquent depiction of a people, a land and a way of life we once knew and loved, and would like to see perpetuated somehow as part of the pattern of our historical and cultural fabric.

I

THE EARLY YEARS

I saw her only that once—a small solid figure standing by herself, self-contained and unassuming. If publicity was alien to her she didn't show it outwardly, though her conversation was shy.

She was all her needlework said she was, a woman who saw into the secret corners of nature, who glorified humanity and animals with her compassionate love, who saw poetry in all things and translated it into every wonderful color there is.

As with persons of latent genius whose powers seem to have been in full flower since they were born, one asks, "Who was she?" Judging from the great beauty she spread forth for all the world to feast upon, she was surely what most of us would like to be—one who fully shared her treasure, a universal voice, a human soul fulfilled.

RUTH BUOL
internationally known jewelry designer and artist,
owner of two Mood tapestries, Carmel, California

Martha, Gus and Helen Wagele (left to right) form an endearing group in an early family portrait.

Martha Mood was not only an artist of stitchery, she was an "artist of life." As Marjorie Guillory, art teacher in San Antonio, puts it, "She could fit the pieces together in life as well as in stitchery." The multiple sides of her being—physical, emotional, mental and spiritual—were in remarkable unity.

The awareness that illuminated her art also united her with people, as a treasured friend and teacher. Once having experienced the love, the teaching, or the art of Martha Mood, one was on a different plane, more sensitized to a sunset, a work of art, other people. She had the ability to transmit her perspective to others, sometimes even to the point of transforming their lives. Almost without end, there appears yet another intimate friend who speaks of her with reverence, joy, and a profound feeling that life has been enhanced by the fact that Martha Mood once trod this earth.

Martha's ability to sense with the intuition of the child was never restrained or trained out of her. We have all had the experience (or heard of it) of seeing a child instinctively recoil from evil, or fly toward warmth and good. Martha had this kind of insight throughout her life. Nor as an adult did she lose her childlike qualities of optimism and ecstasy, which made up a great part of her power as a person and artist.

Her younger sister, Helen Del Tredici, a tutor and former schoolteacher, recalls that from the beginning Martha was attuned to people and her environment. "She noticed things that I never did," Mrs. Del Tredici says, "about our parents, or friends, and would get to the core of the personality, good or bad, and point it out."

August Wagele, Martha's brother, a retired banking official, says:

I remember how much she saw that I was not aware of. No matter what she looked at—in the garden, the sky, or in the house—she saw beauty everywhere.

As a girl she exasperated her father when she picked up a handful of soil and exclaimed, "Isn't this dirt gorgeous?" This quality of responsiveness to all things sentient and nonsentient was to remain with Martha for the rest of her days—equally evident in her art as in her life, for with Martha these were inextricably intertwined.

A rich heritage provided Martha with a source of strength and inspiration throughout her lifetime. Her father, August Wagele, a German immigrant, gave his children this philosophy with regard to achievement: "If someone else can do it, why not you?" Both parents, the father particularly, encouraged their children, built up their confidence, and gave them freedom to grow and move in many directions.

At the same time, from the beginning there existed in Martha a contradiction never fully resolved—a sense of rebellion coupled with a passionate desire for approval. There was a duality in her emotions about her family that might have stemmed first from embarrassment about the earthiness and directness of her parents, then from her guilt about having such feelings. Along with her sensitivity to beauty, she was also more sensitive to hurt. "Mama would say things that bothered her that I wouldn't even notice," Helen says.

Martha developed a pattern of enormous accomplishment quite early—as if time were limited and every minute must count— a drive sometimes laughingly referred to by Martha as "the Wagele curse." Both parents were workers; the father had great drive and determination and did everything at great speed. The mother always kept her hands busy, and Martha's sister and brother are said to be people always on the move. With Martha, the "curse" was a blessing in that it served her magnificent art. But because work was an offering of love, she had difficulty charging for her creations.

Martha drew on her background constantly and was much drawn to it; these were her roots, her very being. As it developed, the family was a root tree for a flowering of talent which has continued into the present generation.

Martha's father, August Wagele, was born in a small town in the Black Forest in Germany. His parents, Appalonia and Jacob, immigrated to Dry Creek Valley, Sonoma County, California, when he was about twelve. By the time the family arrived in America their sponsor in the new country had died, leaving the newcomers completely on their own.

August started assuming responsibility at an early age. He worked on farms, and at the age of approximately fourteen went with an older brother to San Francisco where he found a job in a bakery.

Martha's mother, Martha Glaser, came from a fairly well-to-do family which lived near Stuttgart, Germany. Her parents, Frederick and Katherine Glaser, sold their farm because of the illness of one of their sons, and also moved to Dry Creek Valley, where they bought a good-sized ranch. The sick son, Martha's uncle, who later died of tuberculosis, was the artistic member of that generation and did needlework as he lay in his sickbed.

It was in Dry Creek Valley that August Wagele and Martha Glaser met. They married in 1905 and moved to Oakland where August was to form a bakery business with his brother Fred. "Gus" was the only one of his family of three boys and one girl who did marry—he was the sparkplug of the family, his energy spurring the others on to accomplishment.

August and Martha Wagele's three children, August, Jr., Martha, and Helen, were born in Oakland, Martha on June 21, 1908. Martha had great admiration for her father, with whom she shared many qualities. He was dynamic, happy, and greatly loved by his family as well as by outsiders. "Papa" enjoyed people, wanted to please, and could always smooth over troubled waters.

From August, Martha must have acquired her famous generosity.

August's daughter-in-law, Dorothy Wagele, tells this story:

One day I had some fruit which I planned to share with neighbors. While I was sorting it out, Papa came in and said, "Dorothy, don't you know you're always supposed to give the best away?" This impressed me tremendously.

When the children and their mother went on vacation to a ranch, Papa arrived on weekends loaded down with bakery goods, as he also did when visiting friends and neighbors. In this regard Martha was a "chip off the old block," noted for her excursions and arrivals laden with gifts for everyone.

Even when his powers were waning, August Wagele's generosity remained. Meeting a youngster on one of his walks, August would invariably feel for a coin. His grandson put pennies in his pocket every time he went out so he could have something to give the children.

Martha's feelings about her father are expressed in a letter to her aunt, Annie Wagele, at the time of August's death in 1962:

. . . Papa I know has a treasured place in heaven. He has always been a saintly, guileless, utterly unselfish, loving person and belongs so completely with the angels . . .

Mrs. Wagele, a gentle and loving person, concentrated on making a comfortable and attractive home for her family. She collected art objects and did a great deal of knitting. To her daughter Martha, creating a beautiful home—like a stitchery in depth—was to become a passion.

As a child Martha thought money unimportant and resented having to work in the bakery during vacations. She would ask her father, "What do you need money for?" His answer was, "Just wait until you don't have any." Martha's parents were always concerned about her financial security and tried to make what provisions they could for her. In later years, Martha was to make money through her art, but it was never an objective with her.

In 1915 the opportunity came for a better business in Marin County, so the Wageles moved to San Rafael, where Martha spent the rest of her childhood. With her sister Helen she attended a parochial school, St. Raphael's, and the Dominican College High School.

The early years of the family had not been easy, but by this time there was some money, and August Wagele wanted his daughters to go to a fine school. Unfortunately for Martha, many of those attending Dominican were boarding students from wealthy families. Martha was always aware of the fact that she came from tradespeople with a peasant background; she did not "belong" at Dominican. As a non-boarding student, she ran errands on the outside for the other students in an effort to gain acceptance. The patterns that were formed here probably colored Martha's relationships throughout life.

August, the brother, played the piano, as did Martha. She also enjoyed singing and art. All the Wagele youth were involved in some kind of sports. The sister, Helen, had always felt jealous of Martha because of her many talents. In Helen's mind at least, Martha was the pretty one, in addition to being two years older and popular with boys. It seemed to Helen that Martha was always being shown off. They had never been particularly close.

One night when Helen and Martha were about thirteen and fifteen, respectively, they were in bed talking and engaging in what they called "the truth treatment." Helen said, "I'm so jealous of you." Martha's response was to laugh and say, "Oh, don't tell me that. I've always been so jealous of you because everybody likes you." After that the sisters had a new closeness.

Of college age, Martha attended the University of California at Berkeley, taking off a year to study at the California College of Arts and Crafts, Oakland. Her brother Gus, who had gone to work for a year, started Berkeley at the same time.

Martha was exploring avant-garde movements, and people of diverse backgrounds streamed into the house. Martha's great act of defiance was to wear a long black cape to school, much to her mother's consternation. Outwardly a Bohemian, Martha was fairly conventional in her life style, since she lived at home, as did all the Wagele offspring while attending university. The father had retired at 45, sold his bakery, and literally moved the hearth and home to Berkeley so that he and Mrs. Wagele could be with the children.

The day she graduated from college with honors as an art major, Martha married John Homsy, an electrical engineering student of Syrian background. His ancestors, Martha confided to her sister-in-law Dorothy, had, romantically enough, been sheiks. John came from a large Catholic ranch family in Fresno. There was a great deal of brilliance among the children, particularly in technical abilities. John also had a deep appreciation for music, as well as for Martha's creative endeavors.

The young couple married in the Catholic Church primarily to satisfy Martha's parents. But that was as far as they went, disappearing at the wedding reception before the food was served or the cake cut.

Things did not start out well. They spent their honeymoon at the Russian River, crowded into a small room in Monte Rio, California, along with Martha's usual "seventeen suitcases." John promptly came down with the flu.

From the beginning there was a conflict about money. Martha's approach to this subject had changed little since childhood days. John had a less extravagant view.

The couple moved to their first home in San Pedro, California, where John was assigned by his employer, the Federal Communications Commission. There they lived for nine years and their two daughters were born—Ann in 1933 and Susan in 1935.

Life for Martha was filled with raising her family and producing art. She made toys for her daughters because she wasn't satisfied with what was available in the stores, then found herself in the toy business. The wooden toys were of exquisite quality with wonderful colors— blocks decorated with artichokes and other vegetables, toy boxes, crib figures, jigsaw puzzles.

This is also when her photography began. She became deeply involved in nursery schools because of her daughters and, as Martha

Martha as a young college freshman.

Homsy, did the photography for a book, *Parents and Children Go to School*, by Dorothy Baruch, a personal friend.

The family left San Pedro in 1940 when John was transferred to Honolulu, in time to live through the Pearl Harbor attack. By then the marriage was on shaky ground and Martha looked forward to life in Hawaii, hoping the change would help.

During her Hawaiian stay, she became proficient in pictorial and portrait photography, participating in at least five photography books on Hawaii, including one on hula dancing. They were very popular, especially among the many servicemen who were there following Pearl Harbor. Her photographs were sensitive and technically excellent, reflecting her interest in nature and people. She was fascinated by the weathered old faces of those native to the Islands—fishermen, workers in the fields, children, young people, dancers. In Hawaii she also did a great deal of singing before audiences.

It was here that Martha and her husband met Beaumont Mood, a photographer who was in the armed services. Beau left Honolulu to go on the Okinawa operation during World War II. Injured and hospitalized on Saipan, he returned to Hawaii after many months at war's end and was shocked to learn that the Homsys had divorced and that Martha and the children had moved to San Rafael.

Money was short, so Martha went to work for a photography studio as a lab technician. Martha's daughter, Ann Woodward, a talented ceramist and public school teacher, recalls an amusing incident from this period. One day it had been raining hard and Martha's stockings were soaked on her way to work. She put them on the drying drum in the lab, along with the prints, to dry out. The drum turned happily along, festooned with prints and Martha's hosiery, when the boss walked in. He obviously had no sense of humor. He fired Martha.

Eighteen months after he returned to Hawaii and was discharged from the service, Beau went to his home in Texas. One day he decided to call Martha. Her life was at loose ends; on an impulse she went to Fort Worth to visit him. As he puts it, "a romance developed," and they were married. Martha and the girls moved to Dallas, Ann living with Beau and Martha, and Susan moving in with her father, who had remarried and was also living in Dallas.

Creatively Martha was in a hiatus for about two years, returning to photography half-heartedly. She had become a published photographer; the goal was attained, and now she was searching for something else.

Then one night, shortly after they were married, Martha and Beau were taking a drive when their automobile crashed head-on into another vehicle. The dashboard clock was torn loose and flung into Martha's face, causing severe injuries. She was rushed to a hospital, where doctors performed emergency surgery in order to save her life.

Recovery from complex injuries to her head and mouth took many months in the hospital. For more than a year, Martha wore a mask over the lower half of her face while undergoing repeated operations. She did not tell her California family what had happened, but eventually her former husband told the relatives about the accident in order to prepare them emotionally before seeing her.

Although the plastic surgery was quite successful, Martha's face

Following plastic surgery, Martha regained some of her former attractiveness.

was radically changed. Many of her San Antonio friends, who knew her only after the accident, speak of her beauty, but prior to the accident she had been considered an outstanding beauty.

Because she was used to the adulation offered in response to her physical attributes, Martha must have gone through an ordeal. But she was able to use even this experience as part of her personal growth; it was painful, but it was part of her life. Her beauty survived, but in a different form.

The Moods, having no medical insurance, were forced to sell their home and move into a large apartment complex. The $10,000 bill for plastic surgery kept them in debt for about six years. As soon as Martha was well enough, she did odd jobs to help with the family budget—as a food demonstrator, a saleswoman in department stores at Christmas. None of the jobs lasted long.

Martha again demonstrated the drive, determination, and plain "guts" that had seen her through the bad times of her life—the qualities so reminiscent of August Wagele.

In 1946 Martha started taking ceramics lessons from a hobby shop in Dallas. Beau had been employed as a photographer, and when Martha inherited some money from one of her relatives they used it to set Beau up in a photography business.

Martha and Beau moved to San Antonio in 1952, while Ann went to college in Austin. Martha was to live in San Antonio for twenty years and while there find the richest period of her development as an artist. It was there that she put down roots, became a part of the country and its people, and made friendships to last a lifetime—and beyond. She was also to be a recorder and interpreter of Texas life and of the countryside from which she drew much of her inspiration.

II

SAN ANTONIO

I noticed this small cottage across from the Junior League Bright Shawl tearoom with interesting pots and ceramics in the garden and windows. When I strolled across, there was Martha, who said she was working in clay and wanted to do stitchery. I believe that I have one of the first.

The first commission she did for me was drawn from some small carved heads I had acquired for the Mexican theme of my house, incorporated into a nativity scene against a lovely blue background. It was the most amazing creation.

You were attracted to her the minute you met her—she was such a marvelous character, with warmth, compassion, charm, and intelligence. Her philosophy was love of everything—every human being, every creature. You were also immediately aware of a great strength in her.

RAMONA SEELIGSON
Stitchery collector, San Antonio

The sunroom-studio on Augusta Street.

In San Antonio, Martha found a nurturing and stimulating artistic ambience. As she pointed out in a newspaper interview in 1965, the area offered more opportunities for artists and artisans than many parts of the country. For a long time the social and cultural core of the city had been a group of well-educated, affluent families whose daughters were usually sent to eastern institutions for their education. Through this exposure they returned to become an influence in the regional art world. Martha gave much credit to these women for the growth of local art.

One of the women in the San Antonio art scene was Marion Koogler McNay, founder of the McNay Art Institute, housed in her mansion upon her death in 1950. She bequeathed her collections of paintings, drawings, and sculpture, her residence, and a major portion of her estate to create a museum of modern art. The San Antonio Art Institute, a teaching institution, is located on the McNay grounds. It was at the McNay that a posthumous show of Mood stitcheries and the Portuguese tapestry translations of her work took place in March, 1976—a symbolic return of Martha Mood to the home she loved.

Also in the Alamo city is the San Antonio Museum Association, the umbrella for three museums—the Witte Memorial Museum, the San Antonio Museum of Transportation, and the San Antonio Museum of Art. The University of Texas Medical School has a significant gallery, and banks, libraries and other institutions sponsor art shows in this art-oriented city.

During her lifetime Martha had three shows at the Witte. She also received recognition from the Craft Guild of San Antonio, the Junior League of San Antonio, and the San Antonio Art League. The Southwest Craft Center, Creative Art School, was the recipient of her studio material. Martha's involvement in the art life of the city is further testified to by a Memorial Fund established in her name by The Fiber Designers of Texas (formerly Creative Stitchers of Texas), whose chapters in San Antonio, Houston, and Dallas have members numbering in the hundreds, some of whom had studied with Martha or been inspired by her work.

The resident architects, part of the regional art movement, used Martha's work in their projects. Martha's ceramics career also started in San Antonio, encompassing free-standing sculpture, architecturally functional pieces such as bas-relief and figures, and pottery. Her work was distinguished for its strength and originality. First with sculpture and later with stitcheries, Martha Mood was unquestionably part of

San Antonio's art movement and one of the contributors to its stature and fame.

When Martha came to San Antonio her fortunes were probably at their lowest ebb, barring the time of the automobile accident. When she finally obtained a position at a local school, she had to borrow the money for the filing fee.

Martha and Beau lived on Augusta Street, across from the Junior League tearoom, The Bright Shawl, for about eight years. Their landlady was Caroline Maessen, who lived next door, and the neighbors often ran back and forth to visit and chat. Mrs. Maessen, fascinated with Martha's activities, played an active role in introducing the artist to the San Antonio community. In 1963 the Moods moved to a split-level home on Broadway with more studio space.

The outpouring of Martha's work was not restricted to the plastic arts. An inspired teacher, she conducted art classes in public schools for several years and sculpture classes at the San Antonio Art Institute. She had a popular children's sculpture class at her own studio. Martha had an intuitive sense of what children would respond to. Her school manuals were highly creative, well written, and demonstrated her understanding of art history and aesthetics. She also taught metalwork at a polytechnic high school.

Her advent into the commercial world began when architect O'Neil Ford called upon Beau and Martha to complete a contract for lighting fixtures for the Texas Instrument Building, started by a sculptor who had defaulted on his agreement. The Moods established their architectural lighting fixture business, which was a great success and which Beau continues to this day in San Antonio. In addition to the fixtures, the Moods created fountains, sculptured murals, pottery, and figures. Martha did the designing and Beau the production—the critical shaping of the molds, working with the clay, firing, and glazing.

Recognition by O'Neil Ford was important in Martha Mood's career. A pioneer in the architectural world, Ford was initially called to San Antonio in 1938 to supervise the restoration of La Villita, an old section of the city, a project that was the start of San Antonio's renaissance. Responsible for the design of numerous outstanding schools, churches, commercial buildings and residences in Texas and elsewhere, he also designed the Tower of the 1968 HemisFair International Exposition in that city. (A high spot of Martha's career was the creation of her monumental HemisFair stitchery, depicting the city of San Antonio, for that same Exposition.) Ford in 1976 received additional prominence by being named a "National Historic Landmark" by prominent members of the American art world.

There are certain correspondences in the careers of Martha Mood and O'Neil Ford. He was one of the first to recognize her ability and use her work in his buildings. Ford obviously has his roots in Texas, and his work grows out of the area's traditions, as well as worldwide sources. Martha was also nourished by the Texas soil and implanted in it, even though she came to San Antonio as a mature woman. Wanda Ford, O'Neil's wife, was a close personal friend of Martha's, and active in the movement to preserve San Antonio's heritage and in the arts generally.

Ford was so pleased with the Mood fixtures that he commissioned others for numerous of his firm's buildings. Recognition by other architects resulted in commissions for the New York University and other well-known buildings.

Martha's involvement with people and objects served her new art well—her explorations led her to new buildings, kept her in touch with developments and in communication with architects, who gravitated to the studio to commission fixtures.

The transition to stitchery came in 1959. Winnie Noah, initially a student of Martha's who later worked with her on stitcheries, says:

> *Stitchery didn't come into her life until she was ready for it, and then it came like a bombshell. She exploded. It was marvelous to watch. Everyone was carried along by her momentum. I had been in England for four years. When I returned, we weren't on the phone a minute before Martha insisted that I rush right over.*

Putting aside children and other considerations, Winnie went to the house on Augusta Street where a worktable had been set up in the front bedroom. Martha, in a state of excitement, said, "Look what's happening!"

Architect Ford, who followed Martha as she made the transition from one medium to the other, says, "When she started stitchery I realized that here was a unique artist."

While Martha continued her other arts—teaching, sculpture, ceramics, photography—stitchery immediately became a powerful force in her life.

The impact of the many sculpture and stitchery workshops Martha conducted throughout the country is still felt. She went to New Harmony, Indiana, at the behest of Jane Owen, whose husband, Kenneth D. Owen, is one of the descendants of Robert Owen, who initially established a Utopian colony there in the 1800s. Jane Owen met Martha early in her stitchery career, during the artist's "angel period." As the friendship ripened, Mrs. Owen invited Martha to New Harmony to give stitchery lessons to high school students, and commissioned a lighting fixture for a New Harmony building.

Martha took a memorable trip to New Harmony with her daughter Ann and her nephew Bobby, son of Helen and Walter Del Tredici. Jane Owen offered a house to the visitors to stay in as long as they wished. "You would have thought I had given them the moon," Mrs. Owens says. "Actually they were giving to me."

Martha's daughter was thinking out some problems and Bobby was having conflicts with his calling to the ministry. New Harmony was the perfect place. Bobby is said to have some resemblance to his Aunt Martha. An artist who later taught photography, he has also been on a spiritual search. One of the family stories concerns a conversation Bobby had with his grandmother, Maria Bacci, Walter Del Tredici's mother. The grandmother expressed to Bobby her view that Martha had exceptionally good taste. Bobby's response was, "Noni, that's like saying *God* has good taste!"

Jane Owen re-emphasizes Martha's quality of giving:

> *I don't think she was even aware of how much she did for others. She gave me a sculpture—it was a contemporary Madonna and Child, not a pious Madonna, just a healthy, proud country girl with her baby.*

If Jane bought one art work, Martha gave her two. Once Mrs. Owen told her, "Now Martha, you have to live in the world and pay grocery bills. You must stop giving me things, as I can afford to pay for them."

One stitchery Martha sold her friend for a small sum—depicting a Mexican mother and child—was later burned in a fire. The background was an old army blanket. Martha reasoned that her materials cost her almost nothing; she underestimated her own talent.

Jane Owen comments on the period when Lester Henderson entered Martha's life as her agent and specifically on the later time when the contract included a regular monthly payment:

> *Artists need someone to do this. It's not unlike Father Louis (Thomas Merton), who wanted a little shelter away from the main monastery, where he could write. Without this, Thomas Merton might have been lost to the world.*

On another trip to New Harmony, Jane took Martha to an Illinois farm picnic in the back of a truck piled high with hay. When they arrived there was a rather formal buffet set up at a restored antebellum house. But Martha never really melted until they discovered an old barn and climbed up to the loft. Light was coming through knotholes in the pine boards and they likened it to a cathedral.

"Jane, this is where we ought to bring our prayers, and food," Martha told her friend. So they returned after dark with some of the children, and lay back in the straw in the June night, with fireflies hovering all around. Mrs. Owens recalls:

> *The stars were very low that night. We laughed and we sang and we felt. We didn't know where the stars began and the lightning bugs left off. This was the kind of party Martha loved. She was continually laughing and merry, much as in the adage of the young Christians who were always conspicuous by the lightness and joy in their faces.*

Martha returned to visit the little village of New Harmony and the "open church" designed by Philip Johnson, which Jane Owen had commissioned. Two of the girls she had taught had won top awards at the Indianapolis State Fair and gave credit to Martha.

"I would sum up my contact with Martha by saying that she was an endless pitcher of milk—her supply never gave out, either in friendship or inspiration," Mrs. Owen concludes.

Julia Black, a painter, reports that shortly after she moved to San Antonio, she was driving down the main street and in Frosts Department Store window saw a compelling work of art. Even a fleeting

Forest Scene, stitchery

glance so impressed her that she stopped the car, despite traffic, and backed up to get a look at it.

The stitchery in the window was "Wedding Party," owned by Mr. and Mrs. O'Neil Ford. Mrs. Black decided to learn more about the artist, so asked Lessi Ellen Culmer, vice president of Frosts and a former art teacher, about her. A few weeks later she called on Martha, later becoming one of her assistants.

When Julie decided to go into stitchery, Martha was generous with her time and suggestions, and made her house and her wonderful library of fabrics and threads available. "Mine were in no way copies of Martha's work," Mrs. Black says. "That was the first thing she taught me: never copy anything."

After eighteen years of marriage, Martha and Beau one day came to the end of their relationship. It was a stunning blow to Martha and initially she seemed crushed by it. In typical fashion, she left the home and studio where she and Beau had both worked so hard and started out again alone.

Moving in with a friend for several weeks, she found it difficult to work. It was then that her wonderful friends, Jean Cauthorn and Martha Fuller (owner and business manager, respectively, Cauthorn's Gifts and Flowers, long-established San Antonio shop), offered her the property at Helotes, Texas, on which to build a home and studio. Martha moved out there at once, living in a small stone house already on the land.

Somehow, throughout Martha's life, when she needed something, including people, they seemed to appear. The influence of her friends Martha Fuller and Jean Cauthorn in her life, first with encouragement and support and later with a place to live and work, was extremely important to Martha's life and art. They helped her achieve what was to be the finest period of her creative life—in Helotes.

The building of the house at Helotes was a creative act—and a therapeutic process that consumed her entire being. In a sense, it was her salvation. Martha's daughter, Susan Bragstad, later a successful architect in San Francisco, was visiting San Antonio at the time with her husband, Jeremiah Bragstad, a photographer. Martha asked her daughter to design the house. Susan studied the land, and when she returned to her job in San Francisco at Wurster, Bernardi, and Emmons, she drew plans and mailed blueprints to San Antonio.

As always, Martha worked at fantastic speed. She was impatient to get things done, a characteristic Susan feels she has inherited, undoubtedly another case of the family "curse." Even mealtimes were hurried. They would spend several hours preparing a delicious repast, and it would be gone in minutes.

Martha and Jean Cauthorn scurried around to all the buildings being torn down for the San Antonio HemisFair, and rescued some classic doors, stained glass windows, floor tiles, and other historic objects. Many were incorporated into the design of the new home.

Creating the house and studio was a cooperative effort. Susan would make a suggestion, such as painting the ceilings in stripes. Martha was quick to see the value of the idea, and each room was treated with striking ceiling stripes in different color combinations.

Corrida, stitchery

Mexican Wedding, stitchery

Susan, Martha's daughter, and Martha, working on a stitchery, Helotes, Texas.

In her habitual excursions, Martha found some old floor tiles and brought them to Susan with the comment, "I don't know whether we can use these." Susan greeted the contribution enthusiastically, and the tiles were laid on the kitchen, dining room, and bathroom floors, creating a weathered look. The house reflected both Martha's and Susan's creative ability—the art of putting elements together in a harmonious composition.

The budget, originally $5 a square foot, eventually rose to twice that. Problems came up because Martha did not know how to read architectural drawings and had no experience supervising construction workers. There were frantic phone calls between San Francisco—2,000 miles away—and San Antonio. The end result was well worthwhile, although Martha would not have wanted to repeat the experience.

It was a high-powered team—Martha with her talent for art, color and design, and Susan, who was to become the designer of numerous outstanding buildings in Northern California and receive national awards. A third member of the crew was Ann Woodward, who also inherited a talent for art from her mother and who created the hanging ceramic lighting fixtures for the house.

Qué Lastima, the Helotes home, was an ideal setting for Martha and was featured in a 1974 *House and Garden Guide* after her death. *Qué Lastima* (what a pity!) was the name Martha Fuller gave to the Helotes property when it was first purchased, because of its somewhat desolate appearance. Martha Mood made a paradise of it and there she flourished.

Azul-Azul, stitchery

Country Council, stitchery

Living room of *Qué Lastima,* at Helotes, shows fireplace wall, which extended the entire length of the house. Fidelita, Martha's cat, and her grey poodle appear quite comfortable here.

The kitchen and dining room at Helotes featured bright colors, natural wood walls, and colorful tile.

Papagayos, stitchery

Abstract, stitchery

MADONNA IN BARE FEET

Mandolin Girl, stitchery

We are happy and very healthy and very, very thankful to the dear God for all his wonderful blessings. It seems that each day I come a very little bit closer to God—but it is never close enough. It is so clear to me now that nothing is ours—possessions, money, clothing, children, health, talent, strength, understanding, beauty—everything is God; everything is a part of God; everything is given from Him and must return to Him. We are all one, our only language is love, and, for me, nothing else is important.

MARTHA MOOD
January 25, 1950, Germany

Martha looks lovingly at her Pekingese, whose favorite resting place was among the stitchery fabrics.

Martha Mood was an artist and a force of such magnitude that not only her art, but her spirit, lives on. She reached aesthetic and spiritual heights, yet there was a humanity about her that made her recognizable to countless numbers of people. It was her human qualities, in addition to her art, that aroused the fervor and interest of so many. It is as difficult to delineate what it was that made Martha Mood extraordinary as it is to grasp a sunbeam, yet few exposed to her physical presence, her art, or her essence would challenge the idea that she was a very special person.

While Martha was alive, she would not have been termed a celebrity, yet she is known in places as widespread as Winter Park and Maitland, Florida; New Harmony, Indiana; Corpus Christi and Dallas, Texas; Penland, North Carolina—across the nation. Wherever she went she left her imprint.

Her life was crowded with people, but Martha also enjoyed being alone. When she went to Winter Park for workshops, she was a familiar figure walking up and down the avenue by herself in the afternoons. It gave her needed time to think, to meditate, to get in touch with her creative wellsprings.

Martha's face went through a transformation from her accident. Yet when people who knew her mention her beauty, her flaws—and certainly there were some—are barely mentioned. Her eyes have been the subject of comment by many. They had a remarkable quality—a penetrating softness and depth—even in a family photograph when Martha was a child, the dark brown eyes seem to jump out of the picture at the viewer. Martha's hair—to the end—was almost black, contrasting with her fair complexion.

Martha's voice was arresting, with its lyric, lilting tones, as if she had some exceptional news to tell you. Everything seemed right in the world when one talked to Martha.

One cannot think of Martha Mood without remembering how she gave to others, not only of her inner being, but also in other ways. Browsing in little stores wherever she went, she acquired all kinds of objects that she thought others would appreciate. When she boarded a plane, one could hardly see her for all the baskets and packages she carried.

Jean Cauthorn remembers a trip to Santa Fe with Martha when Jean had the whole back seat of the station wagon to herself on the way out and on the return trip almost had to go back on a plane, the car was so loaded. On an excursion to Europe with Glasfira Williams, a psychiatric family counselor from Chile who settled in San Antonio, the collecting was so fierce that suitcases were left behind in storage in order to accommodate the latest acquisitions.

Margaret Steele, who worked with Martha, is one of countless friends with mementos of Martha in their homes—all gifts. One was a stitchery made in blue and green, Margaret's favorite colors. She had known the artist only three weeks when she was given some ceramics from Martha's mantelpiece which she had admired. "I learned so much about giving from Martha," Margaret says, "more than from any person I have known."

One day, when Julia Black was having personal problems, Martha went to her house and saw that the garden was in a deplorable state. Shortly thereafter, a big truck loaded with soil backed up to Julie's yard. When she protested, Martha said, "I signed that contract with Lester Henderson and don't have to worry now. This is yours."

When Julie's father died, she left town suddenly. Upon her return there was a fragrant yellow rose bush entwined in the trees over her doorway—from Martha.

"I gave her things I would never have dared to give anyone else," Mrs. Black recounts. "Earth from the Roman Forum where Caesar died . . . leaves from the Vienna Woods."

In her work, Martha wasn't concerned that someone might steal her techniques. She *wanted* people to participate.

A faithful correspondent, Martha kept up many relationships through postcards and letters. She brought little gifts for the children of friends.

Martha gave the greatest gift one can give to another: herself. She listened to whatever her friends had the need to relate. If she was tired, bored, hurt, ill, they never knew. But she was seldom bored; her interest was genuine, and she was too compassionate to dismiss anyone asking for her attention. She was so attuned to people that she could almost read their minds—one had to be a superlative actor to hide his/her feelings from Martha.

To each person, Martha brought something different. Mrs. John Webb of Orlando, Florida, a former student, says, "She is one of the bonuses of my life. It was like standing in front of a great painting—it has presence."

Other significant qualities evident in Martha were her strength and dedication, both to her art and her life. Totally involved in many aspects of living, she never lost sight of her priorities. She set goals and kept schedules as much as possible, resisting diversion.

"She could do anything she wanted to—like hands of steel in kid gloves," Mrs. Webb says. "She could get away from the clutches of someone so tactfully and smoothly one would not even know it was happening."

There was little that Martha was not involved with—from nature to politics. Her curiosity about everything was such that in the midst of a meal or entertaining, she would leave her food or guests to search her bookshelves for the answer to some question that had arisen.

She had an extensive library, not just large folios, but including paperbacks and pamphlets on birds, flowers, and fauna. Hardly an hour went by that Martha didn't look something up in this great complicated library, one of the resources for her work. She was fascinated by research—any kind, on any subject—from books and from people. She looked forward to visitors to bring her information about people and events.

With Martha, life meant experiencing everything fully. She was usually up early and did more in a day than most people do in two—visiting friends, going to art museums, shopping for groceries, buying gifts, writing letters, and at night perhaps giving a dinner party. Because the day had been consumed with all these activities, she often worked on stitcheries long after she went to bed, doing the creative part of her work there. Once for her birthday, friends brought huge pillows so that she could sit up better while working, which she often did until midnight, one and two o'clock in the morning. Later in her life it became more comfortable for her to work in bed because of her failing health.

In automobiles, on airplanes, wherever she was, the work continued. The padded dashboard of her car was full of needles and thread. She got others to drive whenever possible so she could sew.

Home was always the heart of life for Martha. It was from this center that everything flowed—her art, her love, her giving. At Martha's home there was sure to be good conversation, loving friends, music and literature.

Martha's house was well organized. She had a place for everything, from the smallest button or piece of yarn to the jars of seasoning in her kitchen. On the walls and shelves were places for her mementos—of friends, trips, her romance with nature. Everything had meaning, like Martha's stitcheries. Buying or finding objects for her home was a constant occupation. On each visit, friends looked to see what change had been made. The house was a part of her creative process.

When Martha had guests, food was always an accompaniment to the visit. Out of her German background came the idea that the table must be loaded with food. She was a creative cook, and even her table settings were works of art.

Martha's busy hands and heart continued their creation of beauty in the out-of-doors. The first hour of every morning was dedicated to her flowers and plants. One of her friends said, "I never heard her talking to them, but I am sure she must have."

In the yard, quantities of ceramic pots of Martha's own design—in varied colors and shapes—served as planters. The plants responded to her attention with vigorous growth—indoors and out and in a little greenhouse in the yard. Without the least encouragement, Martha would tell visitors about a particular specimen, its habits and attributes. She loved the wildflowers equally well.

To this living kaleidoscope was added the fleet movement of wild birds. There were as many as two dozen at one time in a special cage built off one of her windows. She fed the birds and spent hours watching them.

A Martha Mood house was not complete without a dog. At one time she had two Pekingese who dominated the place. When Martha moved to her Helotes home, she adopted a dog from the animal shelter. She always said that her pets were neurotic, but this one had to be the

A bright corner at *Qué Lastima* incorporates Mood stitcheries and Martha's inevitable dried arrangements.

Martha's desk was a background for her artifacts and a place to carry on her voluminous correspondence.

most neurotic of all. The first thing Dunkel ("dark" in German), a black dachshund, did when friends brought her was to jump out of the car and walk right into the swimming pool.

Dunkel loved the taste of wooden shutters, carpeting—anything that went into a house—but was rarely seen to eat dog food. She adored Martha and went berserk when left alone. But Dunkel had a distaste for cars and howled miserably when Martha tried to take her on a trip. Poor Martha also had another problem with Dunkel, which was never quite overcome. She would walk the dog endlessly at night around the two acres of *Qué Lastima* and not until they were back in the house would Dunkel get the point of the excursion.

"It is curious how much pride people take in having known Martha Mood, comparable only to the pride people have in saying their forebears came over on the Mayflower," Martha Fuller once said.

Martha Mood understood people, saw into them—felt each had a special contribution to make to her. They responded to her interest and to her magnetism like anemones opening in the sea. Whether this affected her family, whether they ever felt that the crowds came first, we can only speculate. When visitors arrived at the studio, the focus was quite naturally on Martha. Husbands, and co-workers as well, faded into the background.

Men, women, and children alike were attracted to her, even people who did not know her well. She projected love, understanding, and warmth. While much of the love she exchanged was non-physical, even spiritual, there was a strong physical side. She loved to touch and embrace. As Lessi Ellen Culmer puts it:

> *She was a calm, female, artistic entity . . . in touch with the relationship between man and woman, woman and child, and the created earth. Sincerity was basic with her. You had a feeling of her dependability and love for you as an individual. I felt one could always go to her and say, I have this problem. . . . She had a perspective that was peaceful and beneficial and sprang from love, like a big, beautiful Mama of the world—a Madonna. I am impressed by her contribution to the world of art, but I think, more important, to the world of people.*

A spiritual person, Martha Mood was always looking at her life experiences in terms of religion and philosophy. Her later stitcheries reveal this interest, particularly one called "Centering," owned by Margaret Hammond, a former gallery owner.

After her Roman Catholic beginning, she later attended the Quaker Church for a number of years, read many books on religion, and had a certain devoutness. For some years she was a Christian Scientist, and when Ed Lehmann came back into her life her search included Zen Buddhism. Toward the end it is said that she reaffirmed her Christianity, strengthening the faith that had always been there, as a support in her fight against the fate that was threatening her. Later, when Martha despaired of winning the fight, religion helped her accept separation from life. In her vigorous years, Martha found the greatest inspiration and consolation in nature, to which she often turned as others would to a religion.

She felt life had a great deal of spiritual meaning, but wasn't able to settle down to a single sect. The search went on. She never quite reached the point at which she was ready to say, "Now, I'm going to rest."

Margaret Steele, a close friend and studio worker, was the person Martha often went to for religious perspective in times of trouble and need. Mrs. Steele says:

> *Martha was so sensitive to God, and yet I think it wasn't until right at the end that she did accept Jesus. We used to have the most wonderful time together because we saw God in absolutely everything that passed in front of our eyes. I've never had a friend with whom I could relate as closely in that regard.*

Julia Black often discussed religion with Martha, although she says, "Neither of us was a religious person in terms of going to church." Once Martha told her that she thought there had been an eleventh commandment. Julie asked, "What is it?" Martha replied, "Thou shalt not fear."

She explained that out of fear grows much that is destructive, including jealousy and greed. When one is fearful about being without food and doesn't trust in the future, one may resort to stealing. Martha felt that God didn't intend people to have fear.

Her tremendous courage undoubtedly grew out of her faith not only in a Greater Power but in her own powers. Through the terror of her accident and the demoralizing effects of two divorces, Martha suffered deeply, then looked up and was able to see the faint light of hope breaking on the horizon.

One of Martha's sayings was, "There is no room in life for contempt, ridicule, sarcasm, or blame," and she seldom belittled people, even those who had wronged her. She was always able to see beauty around her—sunlight on the leaves, the light and shadow in the garden, the rainbows on the rim of her cup of coffee, and translate them into art.

The study of human behavior and emotions, her own and those of others, was an absorbing interest of Martha's. She often turned to Glasfira Williams for exploration of her feelings. In turn, Martha was available to many friends who consulted her frequently about personal problems. Always eager to find the newest book or theory on emotional conflict, she would say to Glasfira, "I just heard about a book by Fritz Perls on Gestalt therapy. What do you know about Gestalt?" She had a passion for learning, and Mrs. Williams says Martha was often ahead of her in reading on the subject of psychology and up-to-date on transactional analysis and other approaches.

Martha was always creating beautiful things out of the simplest elements and performing loving acts. Even when she had little, she took food from her plate to feed starving animals, birds, people—and lived in harmony with the universe. She found beauty in people as she did in nature. Lessi Ellen Culmer says:

She was the essence of gentleness, almost like a saint; no matter what happened or why, she always had an open-minded acceptance, a loving smile, and a sweet understanding.

Her smile was for everyone to share, and seldom left her face. Some say they never saw her upset; however, Martha certainly experienced the deeper emotions inevitable in a complete person and artist. In reality, hers was a stormy life. Margaret Steele says, "Martha has known all the aspects of living. She knew being lionized and she knew the direst of dire poverty." She knew, more than once, the depths of despair. Through it all, she emerged and was often even able to laugh at the bizarre shape of her misfortunes. "I've never laughed as much with anyone as I did with Martha," says Mrs. Steele.

An extra-dimensional person—like someone in a photograph in sharp focus with everything else held back—Martha was also subject to human vulnerabilities. Her human side only seemed to endear her more to others. A brilliant conversationalist with a fine mind, the center of attention at gatherings, Martha could still be the shy figure that Ruth Buol saw in 1967 on the occasion of Martha Mood's first exhibition at the Henderson Gallery.

As suggested in Mrs. Buol's sensitive word picture, Martha Mood, the beaming, exuberant, charmed being, was often tense and doubtful of herself. Usually this was not apparent to any but intimate friends. It was only a mote of dust in an otherwise sunlit scene, and, as Martha has shown us, even dust can be beautiful.

Possibly stemming from her early school and family experiences,

Artist's preliminary sketch for "America's First Families,"
vertical, stitchery.

Artist's preliminary sketch for "Religious Motif," stitchery.

Martha had insecurities that stayed with her throughout life. It seems that as a middle child she had the feeling (true or not) that her brother and sister received more attention and love, and later she felt real rejection in her relationships with people of an affluent background.

Martha had a tremendous need to be loved. She was once heard to say, "I just feel as if I have to make everybody like me." In a casual meeting on a bus, or shopping with people she might never see again, she became involved. She often took the initiative in friendship.

Because of her continual search for love and acceptance, she often covered up her negative feelings, concentrating instead on the joyful aspects of life. She had a talent for being gentle in disagreement. Never overpowering the listener with her opinion, she had an almost magic ability to contribute a new point of view that either resolved the question or gave it a broader perspective. Her reluctance to show anger could have been associated with a fear of displeasing, or losing, the love of those important in her life. In her deeper relationships she often held in feelings, only to have them erupt later in a delayed and compounded encounter. But most of the time, her more somber emotions remained locked inside, a process that must have drained her psychologically, and perhaps physically, as well.

She had a feeling of unease around rich people, and a strong dislike of pomposity and snobbery. Once when a rich customer left the studio, Martha said to Margaret Steele, "You know, Marge, that woman makes me feel as if I were an inferior being," despite the fact that the woman came there for what Martha had to give. Mrs. Steele comments, "For her glorious talent, they came to her doorstep and would have crawled on hands and knees to get what she had." In later years, Martha's view of the rich is said to have tempered somewhat, as she got to know them as clients and later as friends.

Some of her repressed feelings came out in a story, joke, or creative art in which she satirized the stance of those whose behavior seemed artificial. She had a gift of mimicry and could closely simulate the tones and phrases of others.

Whether Martha made a comment upon life in her art is open to question. Her brother Gus, among others, feels that she did what she did to portray beauty and that there was no particular comment, social or otherwise. O'Neil Ford implies that there was such commentary, but always with a loving touch:

"The Mexican Wedding" shows a Mexican family, who make the most of weddings, done up big, yet there is never any notion that anyone is making fun of the situation. It has a kind of whimsy, but is respectful.

"High Society" has that quality. The person who owns it is one who truly understands—socially prominent, but with this wonderful critical notion of all things, including society. Martha was on good ground. If she had done this with certain other people—tried to depict the nature of their lives—there is no way they would have accepted it.

One cannot see a representative sampling of Martha Mood's work without the conviction that she saw and felt the full roundness of the living experience. While she may have been to some a Madonna, she was an earthy one—rebellious, unorthodox, even mischievous. She admired formality, yet protested against it. Attending local art center events wearing outlandish clothes was perhaps just a challenge to the dignity of the occasion, as was her habit of greeting her most distinguished guests in bare feet.

Enid Collins of Fredericksburg, Texas, a fellow artist and teacher, was a great admirer of Martha's work and is the owner of several stitcheries. She knew Martha toward the end of her life, when Martha was encountering many problems. Mrs. Collins notes:

Martha's personal life was full of difficulties. It seemed to me that she escaped into her work, and the result was truly art. I often felt that her work was her salvation—her refuge from situations she was unable to cope with otherwise. I believe that she really found fulfillment in her work. Everything she did expressed an exuberant joy in the beauty she saw all around her. She was truly gifted with a special way of seeing, and she polished and perfected her skills to put what she saw into tangible form, so that others might see and enjoy.

There is no doubt that Martha had more than her share of sorrow and struggle—two broken marriages, a nearly fatal accident, economic crises, an early bout with cancer and finally several years of struggling with ill health before her death. Yet the face she showed to the world and the expression of her art were bright and hopeful.

Julia Black reports that in more than fifteen years of friendship, she and Martha rarely spent time talking about illness or catastrophe. Julie didn't know until Martha died that she had previously had cancer, and knew only vaguely about the serious automobile accident. They didn't spend their time together looking back or concerning themselves with things that were not positive and joyful. Their conversation was often in the realm of philosophy and events. Martha was a person of the present. The past was gone. It had happened, but it was not to dominate her life.

IV

STORY OF THE STITCHERIES

I think that order and discipline are the basis of all art. With Martha, an enormous amount of research went into each stitchery. She sketched out almost everything she did before she ever went to look for material. She knew exactly what she was doing: the way she would fold the materials from the shelves to work was the way a painter uses his oils. She knew exactly where she was going, the color relationships and everything else.

She had little outlines of work and play for herself. I put down appointments. Martha put down exactly what she was to do, who she was to see—a diet schedule, a work schedule, a letter to Ed, prepare supper, embroider, cut and pin a Madonna, all were laid out.

Meeting Martha, you really never caught that underlying structure. I was tremendously impressed. She said, oh, well, I have to keep a little road map to know where I am going, and I haven't been well . . . but she'd done it for years. I thought that the real flowering of her talent was possible because she conserved her energies and designed her time as well as her tapestries.

LOUISE MILLIKAN
Houston, Texas

Martha in front of Helotes house with friends and studio workers, Virginia Smith and Ann Drought (left to right).

THE BEGINNING

She was so versatile, it is incredible that God should have given so many talents to one person," says Martha Mood's friend, Margaret Hammond.

Martha had at least four careers—photography, sculpture, ceramics, stitchery—and was successful in all of them. Another vocation which should be added is that of teaching, which encompassed all of her other arts. She also sang, played the piano and the dulcimer, wrote, and, as O'Neil Ford expresses it, "She was art all day long . . ."

Among Martha's most admirable qualities was that of experiencing to the full each art form and then going on to a new one. One part of her career readied her for the next, with startling continuity.

She became involved in stitchery almost accidentally. She had been looking for a new medium and considered stitchery as much a major art as painting. A book she had been studying described stitchery as an art form utilizing texture and design just as they are used in painting. An interior designer friend who knew of Martha's creativity was closing out some fabric samples. Bringing them to Martha, she said, "I wonder if you could do something with these." Martha started looking at the pieces and thinking about what she might do.

About this time, the mother of Margaret B. Pace, artist and fellow teacher at the San Antonio Art Institute, had an accident and was bedridden with a broken hip. When the patient came home from the hospital, Martha went to her with her stitchery book and a bag of fabrics. Demonstrating the stitches to the disabled woman, Martha hoped to get her so interested she would forget about not being able to walk. Martha arrived with her materials almost daily. Doing a stitchery of her own, she tried to get her student to work on one. The idea didn't take too well with her subject, but Martha was on her way.

Everything that Martha had done before seemed to be in preparation for what was now to become her major work. She had always been a pack rat and a collector of "found" objects to be incorporated into her art or her home. She was able to put things together and have them make design sense—in sculpture, painting, still life photography. When she started stitchery, she carried over the same type of design she had employed in the field of sculpture.

Her first hangings were not true stitchery—they consisted of glued-on abstracts of cloth with no stitching at all. In one of her early shows at the Witte Museum they had to be partially reconstructed to keep them from looking ragged. Then she began to use a little simple stitchery, and later, embroidery.

While her own techniques of appliqué and embroidery were in an embryonic stage, Martha's art was full-blown. Her earliest creations exhibited her remarkable feeling for balance and composition and her mastery of color. Seen in film slide reproduction, where the sewing detail is not too obvious, Martha's stitcheries stand on their own as to form and content alone. The appliqué and the embroidery create an exciting added dimension.

With stitchery, Martha Mood had come into her own. As Elise Jerram wrote in the *Monterey Peninsula Herald*, she "... worked with blazing creativity until her death ... at the summit of her artistry in the medium of 'appliqué tapestry.'"

Martha and the women who worked with her called the wall hangings "tapestries," although technically they would more correctly be termed "appliqué stitchery with embroidery."

Stitchery, while not a new word, has come to have new meanings in today's world. While the word "needlework" is correct as a description of this or any of the needle and thread arts, it does not convey the essence of the creative, experimental work being done today by stitchery artists. This change in usage has been taking place for a number of years, as one can see from Martha Mood's notes written prior to 1972, which appear in the third section of this chapter.

In the more than 500 stitcheries she is estimated to have produced, Martha Mood used every kind of textured and plain material imaginable. Velvet, corduroy and denim were joined in artistic accord. Surprising patches would appear—a piece of army blanket, lace for a skunk's stripe, ostrich feathers, buttons for animals' eyes, or a piece of somebody's old long johns. All types of yarn, domestic and imported braid, thread and twine were used to dramatize the basic appliqué.

What was amazing about her work was its plethora of styles. She did not limit herself to one or two approaches. Her work is sometimes pictorial, sometimes purely decorative. It can be abstract or primitive, or elegant and formal. Her scope of subjects was wide and varied: figures, florals, landscapes, marine scenes, nonobjective designs. She was noted for her treatment of animals—dogs, cats, and creatures of the field and forest. One stitchery, now woven into a tapestry, is a gathering of forest animals termed, "America's First Families."

The initial work was quite simple. One of the first stitcheries depicted the face of a sun. Then the angels started coming and proliferated over a long period of time. When the stitchery started, it quickly took over. For a while she continued with clay and photography. Then she worked more on the fabric, and Beau began to take over on the clay.

She had succeeded in mastering yet another art.

A VERY SPECIAL THING

The following is a composite of accounts of the creation of Mood stitcheries by some of those who worked with Martha in Qué Lastima, *Helotes, Texas, and in previous studios: Mrs. Julia Black, Mrs. Ann Drought, Mrs. Winnie Noah, and Mrs. Virginia Smith. Mrs. Smith, in addition to working on stitcheries, made an important contribution in the management of Martha's business affairs. Margaret Steele was another of the key studio workers whose comments have contributed to the text of this book.*

"What happened around that worktable was a special thing." This statement by Ed Lehmann about Martha's studio has been confirmed by large numbers of people who observed the phenomenon. The women who worked with Martha could not accurately be termed employees. They were part of the tradition of the ateliers of the past, where great artists were surrounded by apprentices and assistants. These were unique women, each with a special sensitivity that united her with Martha in a particular way.

Working with Martha was a sought-after privilege. When Ann Drought, a member of San Antonio society, first visited the house on Augusta Street and saw the stitcheries, she didn't wait for a subsequent visit to ask if there was a chance of joining the group. Martha put Mrs. Drought's name on a list—which included more than half a dozen others who had been bitten with the same enthusiasm.

Before long, Martha phoned Ann and asked, "Were you serious about wanting to work with me?" When Ann said, "Yes," Martha replied,

"Come over on Monday." Mrs. Drought, a stitcher in her own right, was a studio assistant for many years.

"Martha could draw, paint, sculpt, all the necessary ingredients which many artists have," says Winnie Noah, "but she had something the others don't have—a God-given spirit."

Martha had endless ideas. She was compelled to work, loved it, and put out great energy to bring forth her creations. The stitcheries were often very simple. With the exception of "America's First Families" and a few others, there wasn't a great amount of complicated stitchery in them, but what made her work so outstanding were her designs. "One could go to an exhibition and pick out a Mood stitchery from across the room because of the design," Julie Black recalls. "She had a special sense for the right material, color, and form in the right place."

The studio at Helotes was a light, bright, airy room with two sides lined with shelves stacked with fabrics according to the colors in the color wheel. Yarns were put in hanging plastic compartments. A separate rack was hung with bias bindings of many colors, and buttons and beads were kept in narrow drawers in a large sewing cabinet.

Her prime source of fabrics was her many friends—those strange and sometimes ridiculous donations of scraps came from everywhere in shoe boxes, paper bags, etc., scraps of all sizes and shapes. Sometimes she wanted to throw them away, but she never threw them very far. A number of interior designers gave her samples. The bindings and burlap, generally oatmeal or cork color, were purchased outright. When

The studio at Helotes was where Martha Mood created some of her most notable work. Left to right are Virginia Smith, Winnie Noah, and Martha.

Harbor Scene, stitchery

Rooster, stitchery

other fabrics were needed, Martha and a co-worker went to little shops and plowed through stacks of bolts.

In starting a stitchery, the backing was always laid down first—burlap or another fabric, nothing too closely woven, like sheeting—material that would take a needle loaded with wool. A well-worn tablecloth, particularly linen, was considered a good choice. Then the layers were built up on the backing. Occasionally Martha pinned the pieces down, but more often, in the morning, the fabric had been cut and laid out for the assistants to pin down. Sometimes Martha added more pieces in preparation for basting, removed pieces, or moved them as she went along, building up her work.

Her technique encompassed two layers of appliqué, the first which she called the background, and the second which was termed the foreground. She might start with the sky in layers, so that one felt it retreat into the distance. Different fabric in the foreground, with changing colors, gave additional perspective. At times inspired by a piece of material, a particular texture, she picked out pieces that blended with colors of the original choice.

Piles of material mounted on the table as Martha and her assistants selected fabrics from the shelves—greens, greys, and whites. She shifted the piles of colors, removing one and adding another until finally all the colors worked together for an exciting effect. Sometimes the design would emerge in this process. Winnie Noah recalls:

We would be wading in fabrics. On a hot day we took off our shoes and went barefoot. At times it was absolutely hilarious. Oh, I'm right there now . . . Martha's little Pekingese nipping at my bare feet. Oh gosh, it got so hot in there without air conditioning.

Generally Martha established a theme. However, she worked more than one way. She often did a cartoon, or drawing, of the general theme of the stitchery, but sometimes worked right from her head. With a large pair of shears, she handcut a whole stitchery, having to keep in mind whether the fabric would be turned under or stitched flat—she had a gift for seldom making a mistake.

As one watched her, cutting and appraising, a flower, a rabbit, the head of a woman, or a small child dancing would begin to take shape, and before long, there was an entire stitchery ready to be pinned down. Virginia Smith, who assisted Martha for six and one-half years, says:

> *As lovely as the stitcheries were when they were appliquéd—the colors, the balance, the proportion—it was only when Martha put her hand to them with the finishing embroidery that they would really come alive and jump.*

Martha always did the fine stitching, which was like "painting in thread," using the thread colors to give dimension and an effect of light and shadow. The embroidery was primarily done in different weights of wool yarn—fine yarn from Persia, or yarns from Mexico selected for the intensity and high quality of the colors. Often she embroidered at night, sitting up in bed and watching television. She was virtually never

Summer Bounty, stitchery

Chelsea Flower Girl, stitchery

without a piece of stitchery in her hand. Sometimes she embroidered at the table as her assistants worked on other phases of the stitchery.

Her output was staggering, considering that this is very time-consuming work. Every day or two, when the women went to the studio in the morning, there was a new stitchery laid out on the table ready to be pinned and/or basted. Sometimes two, three, a half-dozen stitcheries would be in progress at once. Martha and four women could work on as many as six stitcheries at one time.

Much of the work was commissioned by people who wanted a particular subject, size, and color selection, but the greater part was designed just as it came to her—birds, flowers, trees, houses, anything that had meaning for her.

When she received an order and color photographs for a commission of Texas ranchers wearing Stetsons, she struggled to please the customer and still satisfy her own aesthetic requirements. She succeeded. Thinking of what the men would actually look like after working under a Texas sun—leathery—she picked out fabric that looked like leather. She used different values for different flesh tones—the girl with the harp requiring a different fabric than that used for the ranchers.

Two of the first commissions that were important to Martha were from the LBJ Ranch and the Greenwood Farm Ranch of the Lewis Moormans, which she worked on simultaneously. Another of her commissions was from a client who wanted a stitchery depicting her daughter's wedding. Martha designed it with the groom sitting on a chair, and the bride's wedding gown was made from material taken from the actual gown, styled exactly like the original.

Other clients had stitcheries made depicting their homes and family members, or an eventful trip, such as a safari. One, evoking a rich and somber mood, was titled, "Signing the Will," and showed the principal figure signing the document, surrounded by his family—a departure from the forest and animal scenes.

Martha did more than one stitchery of favorite subjects. One of these was "St. Francis of Assisi," of which she did a number of versions. Winnie Noah recalls:

> *I was there when she designed the first St. Francis, because she knew I had a special feeling for the subject. We found the fabulous fabric, brown, and the most glorious apple-y green. It was so exciting. Virginia Smith walked in one day and exclaimed, "Oh, this whole room is charged!" It was. At times it would get so electric we would have to stop to clear the air.*

Ann Drought expressed the atmosphere in which Martha and her assistants worked as one of an "aura of creativity, excitement, and fun." The women often shared in the naming of stitcheries, which they discussed as they worked together. They sometimes suggested themes to Martha, which she developed into stitcheries. Their work was not mechanical—it was part of the creative human process that operated throughout Martha's life and art.

Safari No. 1, stitchery

Desert Secret, stitchery

CREATIVE STITCHERY

taken from Martha Mood's personal notes

A new vitality has come into the needle and thread arts. A much wider and richer approach is transforming embroidery into what is currently called stitchery. These approaches are producing as lively and varied an art as any of the long accepted so-called fine arts.

Until recently embroidery has meant either busy work or decorating a functional object—pillow cases, tablecloths, and blouses. Needlepoint, crewel, embroidery, lace-making—long favorite pass-the-time recreation—were a matter of following precise instructions and patterns and even using "kits." The personal creative element simply was left out of the picture.

Now the needleworker has infinite choices in the use of techniques and materials to aim at truly creative and inventive results. The horizons have opened up and freed the needle artist to think and plan in terms of a true art, using all the guiding principles of aesthetics. (All arts are based on certain principles—which include color harmony, unity, balance, movement, rhythm, variety, impact—whether we are talking about painting, music, the dance, or architecture.)

Innovative Wall Hangings

Endless experimentation is going on—stitchery on silk screen and batik, weaving with appliqué or embroidery, macramé with batik, part lace-part embroidery, the use of parts of clothing (denim jeans), incorporation of found objects like beads, shells, bits of grass, pods, wood, metal, wire, felt, leather, cork. There are many innovations, particularly in the direction of three-dimensional effects and in combining and assembling a variety of media.

Special illusions and atmospheric effects are appearing in galleries through use of all sorts of transparent and translucent materials like net, lace, organdy, organza, veiling—overlapping and setting each other off in delicate or bold arrangements.

For three-dimensional work, artists use materials in special ways, as folding into built-up arrangements of bas-relief, padding, or otherwise suggesting depth.

There are no instructions to cover these developments. The artist is on his or her own, and experimentation can be the only approach. But do work for practical durability. Sew firmly and attach for permanence.

The Subject and Sources

Sources for subject matter are infinite. Many artists derive their inspiration directly from nature, observing and taking "notes" from natural phenomena like textures of rock, bark, sand, erosion, seed pods; the shapes and colors of endless objects all about us—shells, leaves, flowers, sea forms.

It is a matter of awareness, of developing the eye to see with new vision and selectivity to find new resources and possibilities of beauty in the most familiar and prosaic scenes. Start observing with

America's First Families, horizontal, stitchery

Signing the Will, stitchery

discernment, and record details of your surroundings. Then extend your ideas to include richer and more varied scenes—children at play, animals, groupings of houses, trees, buildings, harbors, people, landscapes. With care and a sense of discovery look at and sketch their linear qualities, colors, scale, relationships. Start to translate them into the makings of a subject for your stitchery. Observe, observe—quality, richness, and feeling. Make substitutions until all the observed elements become a theme for your design. Emphasize the significant feeling and idea in the scene rather than slavishly copy.

The relationships between all the objects—the surrounding areas, their colors and shapes—make up the elements of your design. Arrange them into a well-thought-out unity where everything feels balanced, rhythmic and harmonious and achieves the ultimate success of your idea. Above all, avoid imitating the style and mannerisms of other artists.

Starting the Stitchery

My approach to making a stitchery is broken down into two parts—appliqué and embroidery. The appliqué is the cut piece of cloth sewn to a background material. Usually, I use a solid background material; then the first layer of appliqué, called the background appliqué; followed by the foreground (or design) appliqué. The embroidery is added later according to the needs of the development of the design, to decorate, emphasize, or outline the subject or idea.

Background Appliqué

When you have selected a color palette to work with, lay small bundles of the fabrics on the backing, with a discerning eye for good distribution and placement of color. Move and rearrange the fabric parcels until you feel you have the best possible arrangement. Then start to cut out sections of cloth, generously, to allow for changing the shape later and turning under edges where necessary. It is best to use your scissors, not draw the shapes, and learn to think of the scissors as your all-important tool. Choose the shapes and colors of these pieces with background in mind—as a foundation for the foreground design later. Arrange, combine, rearrange, until you are pleased with the positioning. Then pin everything in place—using pins generously in the centers and all the edges to insure flat surfaces and to keep pieces from falling off or moving.

This is a basic step in achieving richness and individuality in your stitchery. Don't sew until you are satisfied that the distribution of the shapes, the colors, the sizes and directions of the pieces are right. The key word is relatedness in the total assembling.

Foreground, or Design Appliqué

The foreground is the critical and most demanding part of your wall hanging. This is the step for which all others were a preparation. The stage has been set for your creative idea.

Do you have a design, an idea in mind? Or do you prefer to let the appliqué suggest further development as an abstract of colors, shapes, directions? Again there is a choice of approaches.

You may make cutouts from colored paper to lay on the appliqué to get the feeling of your design and give you freedom to experiment and rearrange until you are satisfied. If you use paper "patterns," be sure to cut the fabric a little larger than the cutouts to allow for hemming or later changes in shape. Don't cut tiny, spindly or unsewable shapes. Legs of birds, deer, etc., are better embroidered than appliquéd.

While a beautiful photo or painting may inspire an idea, at this stage resist the temptation to imitate, copy, or to be too ambitious. One can easily be discouraged if the project is overly intricate, precise, or tries to copy other media. Leave the complications of perspective, realism, scale, shading to draftsmen.

Designing with fabric and scissors is an art sufficient unto itself and presents infinite opportunities to express its own uniqueness. It is best to make and correct mistakes, to experiment, to use your intuition and your own perception. Play with ideas, shapes and colors with as few inhibitions as possible.

The Embroidery

Embroidery unifies and brings the stitchery into a whole concept, adding another dimension which enriches, emphasizes, outlines, articulates, and decorates the appliqué. Color of yarn work is probably the most vital element in achieving a maximum aesthetic effect now.

Use your fantasy in choosing color and texture schemes. Old inhibitions and timidity about color combinations are decreasing, with bold new approaches emerging. Here is where advice, instructions give way to the needle artist's own creativity. So have fun; play with fabrics and yarns; get lost in the adventure of stitches; and fall in love with color.

V

THE EMERGENCE

Martha must have had inside her a feeling that an American Indian had while making a basket, or a Neanderthal man while smoothing a stone. She also understood the most refined techniques of art. I think she spanned the whole thing and knew it all.

LESSI ELLEN CULMER
Advertising Manager,
Frosts Department Store,
and former art teacher in San Antonio

Mood exhibition at the Oklahoma Museum of Art.

In today's world, the artist is called upon not only to create, but also to market his or her wares. It is probable that, lacking financial support, many talents have never even had the opportunity to emerge. Without the subsidy of church, state, or individual patron, the artist, forced to find other means of survival, often is unable to devote the time and concentration necessary to the pursuit of a career in art. Those willing to devote themselves to cultivating the affluent buyer often suffer a depletion of energies and a watering down of creativity in their accommodation to the marketplace.

Martha was not a promoter or an opportunist. She had, however, the advantage of her charisma and drive, as well as her talent. Because of these things and perhaps a special fate, people appeared who encouraged and helped her by purchasing her work and in other ways. But national recognition was slow in coming.

What was probably Martha's first stitchery exhibition took place at Frost Brothers Department Store in San Antonio, which has a group of art-minded executives who have been responsible for furthering the careers of numerous artists of the area.

One of Martha's early shows took place in the empty storage room of an apartment house. The Houston museum had discontinued its practice of exhibiting regional art, making it difficult for artists to obtain exposure in their own city. Mrs. Jake Hershey, a former Fort Worth gallery owner, sponsored a series of exhibitions in an apartment building owned by her husband. There were about eight shows in all, including a Mood exhibition in approximately 1963, combined with a stitchery workshop, at which more than two-thirds of the stitcheries were sold. It was Martha's first Houston showing. There were three Mood exhibitions at the Witte Museum of San Antonio: photography, ceramics, and, finally, stitchery in the Martha Flowers Gallery. Eleanor Onderdonk, artist and then curator of the Witte Museum, was a major influence in setting up the latter show.

About this exhibit someone commented, "It was a heart-stopper. You walked into that place and there was so much beauty you could hardly stand it."

Martha Mood also had exhibitions, primarily of stitcheries, at the Stewart Rickard Gallery in San Antonio. She participated in the San Antonio HemisFair in 1968 with her HemisFair stitchery and other works. Later there was an outstanding Memorial Exhibition at the University of Texas Medical School. In all, Martha was involved in more than thirty shows in nearly twenty cities from Florida to California.

In 1967 Mood earned the "Artist of the Year" award from the San Antonio Art League, the first time a craftsperson had been given this honor. One of her first stitchery shows was held in conjunction with this event at The Bright Shawl, the Junior League tearoom and gallery. It was hung by Robert K. Winn, then art director of the Witte Museum.

Martha won numerous awards for her entries into group shows, but in the main her works went directly into private collections, some important ones. An original Mood stitchery hangs in the Lyndon B. Johnson Ranch in Texas. Other famous purchasers include former Secretary of the Treasury and Mrs. John B. Connally, Ambassador and Mrs. Edward Clark, Mr. and Mrs. Winthrop Rockefeller, Mr. and Mrs. Lewis Moorman, Jr., Mr. and Mrs. Arthur A. Seeligson, Mr. and Mrs. Charles Urschel, Mrs. Walker Buckner, Mr. and Mrs. Arthur Summerfield, Jr., Mrs. E. K. Gaylord, Jr., the John M. Kings, Mrs. Doris Vickers, and Mr. and Mrs. O'Neil Ford. By far the largest collection of original Martha Mood stitcheries is owned by Lester Kierstead Henderson, Martha Mood's agent.

Eventually Mood began to receive the accolades she merited and to be compensated more equitably for her endeavors. Edgar Lehmann, Beaumont Mood, and others have given a good share of the credit to Henderson.

Like Martha, Lester Henderson, who plays a key role in the Martha Mood story, is a colorful character; he complemented and contrasted with Martha, the pair forming a working partnership that was extremely successful. There was good rapport in the client-agent relationship, and, in his métier, Lester proved to be as creative as Martha was in hers.

Henderson not only has the ability to recognize talent, but to present it to others. To quote a close personal friend of his, the late photographer, Wynn Bullock, "He is a man of many talents, each of which he has developed to such a high degree of expertise that he has outstanding success in such varied fields as portrait photography, aviation, and art collecting." He also has an intuitive sense of timing, partly due to his confidence in his own instincts and appraisals and a willingness to follow through (some would say "gamble") on them.

Henderson began a career in photography in 1927, and he has been credited with being one of the early pioneers, if not the innovator, of natural light color photography. Now a celebrity in his own right, Henderson has photographed such families as the Nelson, David and Laurance Rockefellers; the Auchinclosses (the family of Jacqueline Kennedy Onassis' mother); the Saltonstalls; the Cabots; the Lowells; the Mellons; and the late President Eisenhower's grandchildren.

He was at the peak of his photographic career in the '50s when he began to represent the country's top portrait painters. The transition into other fields of fine art was a natural development and he has focused on them ever since.

In 1960, he initiated an unusual marketing approach in the field of art, what later became known as his "art museum on wings." Annually, Henderson makes four tours, piloting his own Cessna 195, alighting in key cities throughout the U.S. for private shows at the homes of illustrious art collectors, as well as at more modest establishments

Lester Henderson is surrounded by his precious cargo prior to takeoff of his "art museum on wings."

whose owners are intrigued with the idea of seeing an art show in their own living rooms. Today, Mood's work (both stitcheries and tapestries) is featured in these showings, which also include other selections from Henderson's collection.

It was in 1964 that Lester Henderson became acquainted with Martha Mood. She had been creating stitcheries for more than five years and had gained a reputation for them in Texas, with sales to leading citizens, architects, and just plain folk. Henderson had seen her stitcheries in San Antonio, Dallas, Houston, and Midland, Texas, for a number of years and knew that here was greatness that had to be recognized. He tracked Martha down and early in 1965 was able to buy the first of his collection.

At this time, Martha had assistants working part-time to help her sew the appliqué on the backing cloth—her income was minimal. A Mood hanging was obtainable at a modest price, hardly worth the artist's time.

After the agent had purchased a number of stitcheries, he proceeded to show them from coast to coast on his yearly trips. Early in his association with Martha, he found her far more interested in producing stitcheries than in selling. She had no idea of the worth of her productions or her return for the hours put in.

Once he had determined the value of Martha's work, Henderson talked to her about a contract and a realistic pricing program. Without an exclusive contract, he could not sell the stitcheries at prices higher than those offered by the artist. Martha, however, wanted to be free of restrictions, and it was not until April, 1967, that she agreed to sign a contract giving her entire production to the Henderson Gallery, with provisions to allow her to produce a few stitcheries for friends. She was pleased with the arrangement, as was her family.

Julie Black says, "When she finally did decide on it, what a beautiful, wonderful thing it was in her life, because it was the first time she had security."

Lester saw Martha once or twice a year in San Antonio, usually for an afternoon, for dinner, or for an evening. Martha went to California for the opening of the Henderson Gallery in Monterey in 1965 (he had previously had a studio-gallery in Carmel) and later for a combined show of her stitcheries in conjunction with the work of watercolorist Donald Teague and Vernon Smith, premiere wood carver. Within a few years, the value of the Mood work increased several times, as she gained greater recognition.

It was during Martha Mood's final illness that Henderson came up with what was a unique concept in the art world. He envisioned and carried out a plan, with the artist's consent, to have the finest tapestries possible woven from her stitchery designs. Today, with the tapestry art again growing in favor, many famous artists are having tapestries woven from their cartoons, but this is the only instance to our knowledge where stitcheries are used as the originals from which the tapestries are then handwoven.

In 1975, three years after Martha Mood's death, with more and more viewers being exposed to her art, requests from galleries and museums for exhibitions began to come to Henderson's Monterey gallery. He set up 38 stitcheries and tapestries from his collection for a

The Mood exhibition at the Charleston Museum of Art, West Virginia.

traveling show, to tour museums, institutes, and prestigious galleries throughout the United States under the auspices of the Association of Science-Technology Centers, Washington, D.C.

A preview of the traveling exhibition was held at Henderson's gallery in July, 1975, during a week-long open house which attracted hundreds of people. The *Monterey Peninsula Herald* gave the exhibit a full-page story. This, in an area where there are some eighty art galleries, was a real coup.

The response was immediate and gratifying; some of the viewers were even moved to tears. Staff members gave short lectures on the art, and the visitors, including art classes and artists, showed the fascination that Mood's art usually inspires. In addition to seeing her work, they wanted to learn everything possible about the artist and her techniques.

"It was a phenomenon that inevitably occurs at a Martha Mood show," recalls Henderson. "There is nothing else in the world like it. People react to Mood art in a manner that I have never seen duplicated."

In September, 1975, the tour was officially launched with a successful month-long show at the Wichita Art Institute. In March, 1976, with a show at the McNay Art Institute, Martha Mood's art returned "home" to San Antonio and to the welcoming embrace of the citizenry. The subsequent schedule included the Rockford Arts and Science Center, Rockford, Illinois; the Charleston Art Gallery of Sunrise, Charleston, West Virginia; the Oklahoma Museum of Art, Oklahoma City, Oklahoma; and the Leigh Yawkey Woodson Art Museum, Wausau, Wisconsin. A permanent exhibition remains on display at the Henderson Gallery, Monterey, California, home base of the Mood stitcheries and tapestries—the only sizeable Mood collection available for viewing anywhere, with the exception of the traveling exhibition.

With the advent of museum shows and the continued presentations of Martha Mood's art by her agent, the number of Mood fans is certain to grow and before too long assure Martha Mood her rightful place as one of America's outstanding artists of the twentieth century.

Hemisfair (section), tapestry

Hemisfair, stitchery

VI

END OF DAY

End of Day, stitchery

Band of Angels, stitchery

I thought I could state easily how I feel about Martha Mood and what she has given to the world, but nothing seems quite adequate . . . I only know that when I think of her I feel a happiness and balance with the universe and a reassessment each day of surrounding beauty—ours for the looking and expressing, each in our own way.

BARBARA M. MEYER,
artist, Orcas Island, Washington

The artist in front of her studio-home, *Qué Lastima*.

During the time her first husband was assigned to Honolulu, Martha had met a young soldier at a Quaker meeting, and there was an affinity between them. As they were both married at the time, they went their separate ways, presumably not to meet again. The young man's name was Edgar Lehmann.

More than twenty-five years after his first meeting with Martha in Hawaii, Ed, by then in the investment business, visited his daughter Marjorie in San Francisco. Marjorie took her father next door to meet her friends Ann and George Woodward. On the walls of the Woodward apartment were Martha Mood stitcheries, and Ed learned to his astonishment that his and Martha's daughters were friends. Learning that Martha was no longer married, Ed, by that time a widower, quickly phoned Martha from Ann's apartment and arranged an immediate reunion.

Forest Families, stitchery

Shore Birds, stitchery

Ed felt as though he could have flown to Texas under his own power, but was hampered somewhat by the late schedule air service. The roses he carried in his arms all the way from California were slightly wilted. The dinner that Martha had prepared for him was a little dry. It did not matter. They met and decided it was finally time to "team up." Ed had recognized Martha's beautiful spirit the first time he met her. It was still there. They were to enjoy a number of good years of sharing, growing, and creating.

According to one comment, Ed is ". . . poetic . . . a beautiful, sensitive person." Like Martha, he was engaged in a search for fulfillment and had the same curiosity about life as she did.

They spent their first summer in Duvall, Washington, near Seattle, in Ed's world. Martha took her stitcheries with her, but focused her attention on her new husband. Living in a rustic ranch house, high on a hill in the woods, they built fires, went to the well for water, fed the horses—it was an extremely private time and they were ideally happy.

Following are excerpts from Martha's letters to Jean Cauthorn and Martha Fuller during this period:

> *Dearest Jean and Martha,*
>
> *I've been missing you very much . . . This is the weekend for your Vancouver trip, no? Why didn't you let us know the name of your hotel so we could have phoned you there? We don't have a phone out here in the country—it's a 10-party deal and completely impossible to get through—so Ed doesn't even have the service. He has a phone in his office in town.*

I have really started to become acclimated to this country living, and am beginning to fit in with the pace, which is quite different. Ed gets up at about six and cuts wood and builds fires in the house, feeds the animals, etc., and I sleep 'til eight or so then get super room service with breakfast on tray. Then Ed leaves for Seattle at about nine, and I take over keeping the fires going. I've learned how to just keep enough fire going all day to keep the house comfortable without having to go out for more wood. At first, I kept forgetting and would have to start new fires, but now I'm indoctrinated.

I go out every now and then and just wander around in the woods or get a bucket of spring water (our well is quite shallow and we drink only the water from the "crick"); mostly though I'm still drinking beer as you might guess.

I've been getting quite a lot of sewing done, surprisingly. It is so pleasant sitting at the big table looking out onto the fields and trees. I've been sending completed pieces to Helotes and the girls are sending their stuff to me to embroider.

Ed and I have had some gorgeous trips to beautiful places and went raspberry picking. I'm going to make some jam one of these days. Sundays here are like Sundays at QL—time for people to drop by. We've had quite a few hippies recently . . . I can feel my mind stretching and flexing and beginning to get into the spirit of things. It's fun!

I simply can't get used to going to bed while it's still light—even in rainy weather it's light at 10.

Ed has been doing a lot of manual (Manuel!) janitor type work

Sans Souci, stitchery

Grape Arbor, stitchery

getting a house and an apartment refurbished for renting and is
finally finished with it, has both rented now and feels a little relieved
and relaxed about the situation.

Jean, or Martha, be a pal and send me a big cloth
black-and-white fish, and a floral catalog if you have one. (Even
though there are a lot of Japanese stores here they only have the
small size fish.)

Also, Jean, among your many cookbooks do you have a small
one that has dessert, especially preserve, recipes? Ed doesn't have
one cookbook and I forgot mine and almost never go to town. I hope
you won't mind sending a parcel—thanks very much, kids.

I went to my first Zen meeting with Ed and was very much
moved by it. I think I will continue going. It's every Tuesday evening
in Seattle—just six or seven people—almost entirely meditation.

I hope this covers our happinessville! Have I neglected
anything?

I miss you and I love you!

Dearest Jean and Martha,

When Ann and George (daughter and son-in-law, Mr. and Mrs.
George Woodward) were here last week we blew the gang to a
glamorous trip up Lake Chelan—a 55-mile boat trip on a lake in
the Cascade Mountains—and spent the night in one of the little
boating resorts on the lake, Cove Marina. It was really fun . . . took
four hours each way . . . a one-hour layover and murderously good

meal at the end of the lake before returning. Ann and I rowed all over the lake but the two chicken men were too lazy and used bird-watching as their alibi.

[Editor's note: Martha writes here about staying home to write to her friends while Ed goes to a meditation session.]

Ed and I have had so many beautiful trips to special places to find driftwood and wonderful wildflowers—we seem equally ready to put off work for fun. Poor Ed, I have this place crammed with seed pods and driftwood and other junk now. He really does love it and notices every little bitty rock and twig added.

Somehow I am keeping up with the work schedule quite well— the stitchery—I can't quite understand it myself. I guess being here alone during the day with no interruptions makes it conducive to working. The days are so long—staying light so long I have several more hours before bedtime, too.

It's still so cool, we have fires morning and night.

The strong need of Martha to continue her creative life to the fullest drew Ed and Martha back to San Antonio.

When Martha became ill, Ed was to prove a stalwart. He had, in a sense, been with her even in the years of physical separation. He stood by her as her day ended.

Martha's laughter did not desert her either. She had a superb sense of humor which came through virtually in the middle of tears. It seemed that if she cried on someone's shoulder, she immediately regretted it and wanted to make that person laugh. Entertaining to young and old, she could keep people delightfully amused for an entire evening—always the center of attraction.

Up-to-date on developments, even in later years she retained her youthfulness and vitality. Keeping in touch with the younger generation, she was always ahead of her own contemporaries.

With her sensitivity, Martha became aware early that there was something wrong with her physically. At least three years before her death, she tried to get evaluations from several doctors, who treated her for obesity and other problems. Through a friend, Richard E. Miller, she was referred to the University of Texas Medical School at San Antonio, where Mr. Miller was director of news and information. There her illness was expertly diagnosed, but it had progressed too far. She went into the hospital in May, 1971. A cancerous tumor and one of the adrenal glands was removed, and there was indication that the cancer had spread.

She had great courage. She and her husband decided to live from day to day.

Ed Lehmann's life was tremendously affected by his relationship with Martha. He comments:

Each day was a special gift. If fate had decided that this disease would cut her life short, then at least each day was to be lived. She continued to work. It wasn't escaping from life . . . her work was her life.

The most wonderful thing in my personal life is the pride that I have that I was able to come back into Martha's life when she really needed me. The contribution I made to her life was on a personal level, but it raised my consciousness and awareness in an unbelievable way. I learned from that experience that it is possible for one human being to come to the aid of another.

Martha's loneliness . . . it's a complex thing, because there is this feeling of being isolate and alone, when disease such as this strikes and a person is helpless in face of it. Her real greatness was in accepting this fate, but still living intensely from day to day. Those days stretched out to more than a year and our relationship became most intimate as we communicated in preparation for her dying. The joy she brought to life, knowing that life was really temporary . . . the intensity of it, with every day a special day . . .

I have this living memory and live my life now with constant awareness of her spiritual presence, not in any far out way, but I am never unaware of this great, loving person that was part of my life. Her love of nature has been transferred into my way of life and today I am surrounded with beauty, flowers and plants.

My friendship with Martha's brother—loving, close . . . he recognized in Martha even as a child a special kind of genius. I think of his loyalty, love and devotion, because Martha was a free spirit and Gus is in many ways a conventional man. An ardent Catholic, he practices his faith, but he was never intolerant of her as she experimented and made mistakes. He called her genius "this gift of God."

Her sister Helen is another beautiful person who has recognized this special quality in Martha down through the years.

Regarding our mutual interest in Zen, what was really involved was the search for greater awareness. Martha's whole work is an illustration of her reaching out to touch life. She had this universal love for people, although there were selected persons that she really became intimate with and who shared her.

My relationship with Martha left me with great appreciation for the privilege I had to be close to this wonderful person. Her life for me in a sense transcended her art. The reality of her life and the spirit she brought to it and to her work was so beautiful that I don't know exactly how to deal with it. It transformed my life.

Martha was able to face the realities of her situation. One day she called her friend Margaret Pace and said, "I know there was a minister that meant a great deal to you when you were having troubles of some kind. Could you give me his name? I've just found out I'm going to die, and I need to talk to a minister."

It was the day before Christmas, 1970. Mrs. Pace got in touch with Reverend Joe Brand, an Episcopal priest. They drove out to Martha's house and spent the better part of the day, Martha and the minister alone. Mrs. Pace felt that he was a great help to Martha. He said, "She certainly has spirit," as they drove back. After that, Martha seemed to accept more fully the idea that she was going to die.

While she was afraid of dying, she rarely showed it. For as long as she was able, she made the effort to entertain whomever came to see her—to laugh, to talk, to share the few good things left in her world. These included the sight and sounds of birds outside her window, letters from friends, contact with loved ones, even TV. No one felt it a duty to visit her, as is so often the case with sick people. It never ceased to be a privilege. Friends were pained at their helplessness to do anything for her, but she always lifted their spirits. Even confined to her bed, she loved to share.

One of her occupations while ill was watching the scene she had created in and around an old window. "If Andrew Wyeth had seen it," Julia Black comments, "we would have had another 'Christina's World.' It was magnetic. The window told so much about Martha, the way she lived and her appreciation of life."

Outside the window she had suspended gigantic pine cones and filled them with peanut butter, bacon, and birdseed, attracting all kinds of migratory birds for her perusal. A perpetual ballet performed in front of her window, with birds floating in to eat. In the window she had arranged a piece of antique lace, and small bottles with weeds in them. There was a miniature, old-fashioned metal stove, like one she had had in the house as a child, along with various other souvenirs. The arrangement was like a beautiful painting.

Lotus was the little dog that Martha Fuller had at the time of Martha Mood's death. Jean Cauthorn and Martha Fuller often lived in the rock house at Helotes on weekends and brought Lotus with them. But when Martha became ill, they left Lotus at home.

On one visit, Martha Mood asked them, "Where is Lotus?"

"Lotus just jumps on your bed and makes so much noise we had to leave her at home," her friends told Martha.

One day she said, "I want to see her so badly."

So Martha Fuller brought Lotus. The sick woman put her hands around the dog, as if to study her, saying, "Oh, little Lotus, you're so cute."

On Christmas Eve, a year after Martha's talk with the minister, Jean Cauthorn and Martha Fuller came to see Martha, who by that time was barely able to sit up. (She was to remain alive until the following July.) Martha had Ed get a stitchery she had been working on—and there was Lotus. Martha had been making it for months in secret. She had a picture of Lotus, and had even sent Virginia Smith out to get a book on the Lhasa apso, so she could get the coloring just right, but since they hadn't brought the dog very often, she had difficulty doing the stitchery. This was Martha's last Christmas gift to her friends—and a touching moment.

Martha's will, and her eagerness for life, must have contributed to her living on for a long time despite an extremely weakened condition. The devotion of her husband, Ed Lehmann, was also a big factor. She was at home until the end, and Ed insisted upon doing every thing for her, far beyond what seemed physically and emotionally possible.

On one of the last days, Mrs. Black was at Helotes visiting Martha, who by then was unconscious. She had gone into the bedroom to see her friend, and, wrapping some ice in a towel, moistened the dying woman's lips. She then left the room. In a few minutes, Ed called her back. He said, "Look at that, Julie." Martha's hand was on the pillow in the most exquisite gesture. Mrs. Black recalls:

It was something out of Swan Lake, that little hand. Even though she was so swollen, and not conscious, there was still a feeling of grace and beauty, which Ed saw and appreciated. He was magnificent.

During her last few remaining days, her brother, August Wagele, and his wife, Dorothy, came to Martha's bedside. Gus began to say the "Our Father," and Martha repeated the words after him. When they finished the prayer, Martha on her own began to say, "I love you, I love you, I love you." She kept this up for a long time. Dorothy comments, "We knew she wasn't talking to us."

As they had been with her in her life, Jean Cauthorn, Martha Fuller, and Ed Lehmann were with Martha during her time of dying—one of them was always by her side over a period of several days until the end. It was not wholly a time of sadness. Martha requested the playing of folk songs and hymns she had heard at the Church of the Redeemer in Houston, a young people's church, which she loved. She was aware of the presence of her husband and friends. There was beauty along with the pain of the experience, but Martha did not accept death with acquiescence. Ed Lehmann says, "She knew death was there and she was pushing it back."

With loving friends and her husband keeping watch and gentle music filling the room, on July 15, 1972, Martha Mood died. The shock of this loss was a brutal one for the many who loved her, but there was, and is, great consolation in her passing: Martha, in death as in life, continues to go on giving.

ADDENDUM

A small group of people sits in a loosely formed circle. The nominal leader asks a member, "Is there anything you want from the group?"

The member, whom we shall call Marie, says, "I relate to John. He reminds me of my father. I would like to have John hold me just as though I were a little girl." Marie sits on John's lap and he fantasizes that she is his child. He murmurs loving words: "You are a beautiful little girl. I love you so much and I am so proud of you." The tears flow. Marie, mother of two children, has terminal cancer.

A short time later Marie phones John and tells him that she has decided not to continue with the medical therapy. "I am going to face up to it," she says. "I know that I am going to die. What shall I do?" John shares his own experience with the loss of a loved one by cancer. "Love your family more than ever," he tells her. "Call in your kids and husband and hug them, and don't be afraid to talk about it."

This incident is based on an actual occurrence in a cancer support group. In Seattle, Washington, today there is such a group called Facing Personal Loss, which was formed by Cancer Lifeline and Family and Child Services of Seattle. This is one of a small number of a similar nature that exist in other parts of the country to give support to those who have experienced the loss of someone close or who are themselves facing a life-threatening illness. This group meets weekly for approximately six weeks, giving participants the opportunity to release feelings, gain perspective, and simply to hold a comforting hand. Other groups choose to spend time in hospitals, or with people facing surgery or other crises in their illnesses, on a one-to-one basis. In some cases, volunteers have no personal reason for becoming members, but simply wish to be involved in a helping way with other individuals. Some groups are operating on the basis that such human help may even result in physical, as well as psychological, improvement.

Ed Lehmann is a member of the Seattle group. He is also a member of Synthesis, which has a program oriented to helping those going through crises of life as well as the crisis of death. For Ed, it is a continuum in the life process that evolved from Martha's illness and death and surely can be counted as another aspect of the heritage of Martha Mood.

VII

TRIBUTES TO A GREAT ARTIST

When Martha started stitchery, I realized that here was a unique artist. She wasn't primitive, but she had a certain naiveté and no interest in clichés or patterns. This is one of the greatest things, because most often a designer or artist is influenced by someone else, and it's evident.

Her compositions were darned good. That was one of her amazing qualities. Some of her work is like a Byzantine mosaic at Ravenna. But she had never paid any attention to Byzantine art. The impulse that gave the Byzantines their naturalness and the simple way they did things was the same one that led Martha to do these things. She was a natural. She was very sentimental about the wedding stitchery, though it was not a sentimental piece of art. It was a natural expression.

She was an artist in the sense that many of the great Renaissance artists were, who went every morning at eight o'clock to paint the altar pieces, as the bricklayers went. She did the same thing—worked for her daily bread.

She insisted on giving me some nativity sculptures which I think are museum pieces. Unfortunately I couldn't buy many of the great stitcheries and panels, but I did sell a number to other people, for so little it makes me cry. It was her rent and food.

She was doing a lot of photography and took pictures of my children which were extraordinary. Every one brought out something in the child that I had not previously noticed. She could have made money as a photographer, and wouldn't, but photographed people she liked to look at. Love was her whole story, love of people, love of what she did. And, of course, she was the recipient of that same kind of love. At that time she was married to Beau Mood, and they seemed extraordinarily happy doing things together and helping each other.

When she did sculptures, there was a certain narcissism about them, I suppose, because they were chunky, the way Martha was. What she did was good and strong. She never gave in to the temptation to be influenced. A great many artists purposely or unwittingly fall into some manifestation of Paul Klee or something that Modigliani has done. Her people are like people. Her cows are like cows.

They lived on Augusta Street in San Antonio and they were poor. I've lived with poor artists all my life. But the Moods gave parties that were the most glorious occasions.

Her lyric voice held you the minute you walked into the room. She was a beautiful person right on through her art. She was art all day long—the damnedest thing I ever saw.

O'NEIL FORD
noted architect, one of Martha Mood's early discoverers
who used Mood stitcheries and sculpture
in many of his buildings

I think that what makes Martha Mood great is the humility of her work. She found beauty in being straightforward and simple, almost elementary, in what she did. What drew me to her work so much was that it had the childlike view of nature—uncontrived, with a marvelous naturalness. There was nothing done to be sophisticated.

Most artists reject society to a great extent and paint this rejection into what they do. So most of it is not very happy art. What was significant about Martha was that she never got back at anything; she was such a kindly person that she could only paint the goodness that she felt.

The thing that always impressed me about Martha's work was that she was a humanist. She saw the innocence of life and did not put into her work anything but the feeling of love she had for nature, its simplicity and colors, and used simple forms to express nature.

Unlike many artists who, after becoming extremely successful, have a tendency to mass production, Martha never succumbed to commercialism. Whatever she did was something she was giving to another.

She did things as she saw them. They were not decoration, but rather an expression. Her hangings were the warm, embracing feeling of the whole area. In my estimation she saved many buildings for architects, because she had a warmth that did something the architecture wasn't doing.

The radiance of this woman for me was that she refused to be stereotyped. She did not manufacture her art; she created it. And she was so prolific. She could work with many different themes equally well. She did the Stations of the Cross, and did that well. She could do flowers in a way that would give you a different impression of the nature of flowers than you'd ever had. Landscapes—tree forms—not all artists can do that. They can either do figures well, or architectural things well. They build their ego on that one thing and are afraid to expand out of it, but Martha was never afraid. She was a fearless artist, because she had it.

ROGER RASBACH
prominent San Antonio designer

For several years I received reports of a remarkable woman in Texas who was doing original stitchery wall hangings. I finally ran across one in a friend's collection and discovered that "the genius of Martha Mood" was true—and understated.

I was very pleased indeed when I found the opportunity to present an exhibition of her work at the Wichita Art Association Galleries. Through the generosity of her friend, Lester Henderson, we were able to exhibit his extensive collection of her stitcheries and the Portuguese tapestries which were being produced from her original designs. It was one of our most popular shows.

Her craftsmanship in textured fabrics and fibers has strong impact on viewers of any age. Her charming whimsical scenes, her sensitivity to style, and her stunning use of color are reflected in every piece.

The designs which have been interpreted in tapestry are equally effective and, gratefully, will preserve for future generations the unique artistry of Martha Mood.

JOHN R. ROUSE
Director and Curator,
The Wichita Art Association

Toucan, stitchery

Martha had formal training, but I think she was born with this talent for seeing and recognizing objects and designs and a way of putting things together that is virtually impossible to teach anyone.

From a standpoint of design, the stitcheries are top quality. Nothing can compare with them. Martha had a sense of color that few people achieve. She was remarkable in that she didn't have a set color scheme, and could go in any direction—any combination she put together was superb. I've never seen anything that was jarring or out of place.

ROBERT K. WINN
former Professor of Art, Trinity University, San Antonio;
former Director of the San Antonio Art Institute;
former Art Director of the Witte Museum, San Antonio;
presently art consultant for leading architects and designers

Martha Mood's art is an eloquent statement helping define the seldom-experienced beauty that surrounds each one of us. That's all it does, and that exquisitely, requiring no more comment than the warmth of the sun. It demands no further explanation or understanding of the head, only the love of the open heart. If it can be shared as simply as she offers it, then the bond between herself and her audience is complete. She was certain that joyous art like hers is always expectant, waiting only to be grasped and embraced. The world she reveals is easy to take. It is a light, multi-colored fantasy of near-plausible images, never dull, never repeated, never completely familiar.

To look at her stitcheries too closely one might be distracted by her sure sense of drawing, the certain touch for color that flames her private world into life. Her transformation of the commonplace into high fantasy can be intriguing, but such questions of technique and execution, and others as well, are less important now; they will be analyzed in time as they deserve.

What remains distilled for those who are enriched by the world she offers is the certainty that if the gentle beasts of her vision, her glowing plants and shining houses, her leaping fish and crimson ships, if all of her world that lives so vividly in her pictured imagination is shared, it will continue to live on for those who care to share her world as I do.

ROBERT A. WEINSTEIN
specialist and consultant in maritime history,
and in the photographic history of the United States

High Court, stitchery

Chickadees, stitchery

Our first meeting with Martha Mood, an unforgettable experience, was at her exhibit held from May 14 to June 4, 1967, at the Witte Museum of San Antonio, Texas, the year she was named "Artist of the Year" by the San Antonio Art League.

After an hour or more spent in absorbing the dazzling beauty of her work and noting the ones available, we pushed our way toward Martha, surrounded by admirers, and were introduced by our long-time friend, Glasfira Orrego Williams. Although weary by this time, Martha was all warmth and smiles as we told her of our desire to own one of her stitcheries, which we had already selected.

We completed a quick financial arrangement and came away, exhilarated and feeling that we had found the pot of gold at the end of the rainbow. We have many paintings and other works of art in our home, but I believe the possession of Martha's "The Ritual" has brought us more pleasure than any of the others.

From that day we began a warm and rewarding friendship and soon thereafter called on her in Helotes, a small resort village near San Antonio where she had built a most attractive stone and timber home on the side of a hill, surrounded by a vast reach of uninhabited woods. The house, designed by Martha and one of her daughters, was specially constructed to meet the demands of Martha's work and recreation. A large workroom was furnished with a central table surrounded by several high stools. Tall shelves filled one end of the room where she kept the hundreds of pieces of materials and yarns for her work. An amusing aside about Martha was that if one was wearing a garment whose color or texture had possibilities of being

incorporated in one of her stitcheries, she might well talk you right
out of it. Many stitcheries, partially completed, adorned the
workshop and spilled into the adjacent large living room, separated
from the workshop by tall bookshelves, filled with a fascinating array
of art books which invited one to linger. Opposite the entrance was a
large stone fireplace surrounded by comfortable sofas and chairs.
To the west of the living room was Martha's tiny bedroom, a bath,
and a combination kitchen and dining area, the latter two filled with
many plants, lovely pottery and many quaint antiques.

The first impression one received of Martha's home was one of
warmth and clutter, but the kind of clutter that, upon examination,
revealed many of Martha's interests, for she found beauty in the
most minute trifle: a bouquet of grasses which the frost had turned
to bronze, a plant which trailed over and around the windows on
either side of the fireplace, a tiny stone picked up on a walk, a piece
of driftwood which had an artistic form, or even a bird's egg of
mottled blue. All of these objects, rarely noticed by most, were
meaningful to Martha, for she had the most sensitive attuning with
nature and all of its small and large offerings. One of the objects I
admired was a basket, filled with pieces of driftwood she had picked
up on the Pacific Coast. Not long afterwards, I received a box
containing exquisite pieces she had selected for me on one of her
jaunts on the beach. Each is a little gem.

Not only was she generous with nature's gifts but with her own
possessions. One day I wore a lavender-pink raw silk suit with a
pearl necklace. She left for a minute and returned with a magnificent

149

June Flowers, stitchery

Shells, stitchery

ceramic bead necklace she had made and whose colors blended with and enhanced my suit.

She and Ed spent a New Year's weekend with us in Muzquiz, Coahuila, Mexico, while we were doing ethnological field work on the Mexican Kickapoo Indians who lived nearby. She was entranced with the Indians, their village, their way of life, so different from ours, as well as that of the Mexicans of our small town, with our adobe-walled house which we had enjoyed furbishing to meet our own needs. Everything was a source of novelty, excitement, and interest. I remember she wasted no time on this trip, for while we chatted in our living room with the warm sun pouring in, she brought out one of her stitcheries and put in the finishing touches.

Not only was Martha an interesting person, but she was interested in everything, a quality possessed by few.

When illness struck her, we all suffered. The months she lived after it was discovered she had cancer were months of agony for all of us. Her decision to stop medication and face death quietly and serenely in her own home with just Ed and a faithful servant to attend her needs was an example of courage to all who loved her and tried to show their devotion in myriad small ways. I remember taking her a dessert of mangoes she had enjoyed in Mexico. She was then so weak that I had to spoon-feed her. With strength she mustered from sheer character, she smiled and smacked her lips after each swallow. Her gesture brought both tears and smiles.

152

Ed was a paragon of devotion. He attended her so gently, made a garden and brought her flowers, vegetables, and nature's little offerings to delight her; supplied the birds with feed at the small window where Martha could watch their comings and goings. Martha's and Ed's life was a romance, a beautiful bittersweet experience which we shared with them until the end.

DOLORES AND FELIPE LATORRE
authors and anthropologists

Safari No. 2, stitchery

The Race, stitchery

I will always remember Martha's magnificent strength of character. Regardless of the setbacks, she continued to create better work until she had reached the heights. Her stitchery and sculpture had a strong emotional and spiritual value in later years.

Her love and understanding of people and their many moods are evident in the portrayal of children at play, wedding scenes, photographers in action, and quiet, pensive portraits. She worked in various media, photography, painting, illustration, sculpture, and stitchery, which was her favorite.

Martha's interpretation of animal life, both wild and domestic, was superb. Stitcheries of small animals in their native habitat show Texas wildlife at its best. It is impossible to look at these without realizing how sincere was her love for God's creatures.

After helping me with my many cats, one summer Martha made a large stitchery of them. It is very dear to me, both because of the excellence of the work and because it shows her love, sense of humor and understanding of the felis domestica calculata *(calculating feline).*

Martha had that rare ability to relieve tension in difficult situations. When we planned to teach together, I ordered a large kiln to accommodate her sculpture, which we found was far too big to go through the doors or windows of our building.

Martha, in her sweet, calm way told me not to worry, some plan could be worked out to get it in. Thanks to a maintenance man, door frames and brick were removed and we had our kiln in place. She could "fit the pieces together" in life as well as in stitchery.

156

Martha Mood was truly a great person in every sense of the word—an artist of tremendous creative ability, a wife and mother with much love and tenderness for the members of her family, and a teacher whose fellow teachers and students adored her. She lived far above us, often cautioning not to place too much emphasis on material things. Hers was a life of kindness, creativity, and love of God and her fellows. I feel I am a better person for having known and worked with her.

MARJORIE GUILLORY
art teacher, San Antonio

Religious Motif, stitchery

One could recall the words of philosopher Walter Russell, who didn't have Martha Mood in mind when he penned this, but he might have had someone like her at the back of his thought:

"He who cultivates that quiet, unobtrusive ecstasy of inner joyousness can scale any heights and be a leader in his field, no matter what that field is. A joy which very few know, and a very few experience, because that joy only comes to the great thinkers.

"To those who do find that inner joyousness which comes from that miracle of discovery of Self which is within every man, comes something also which is greater than success. To them comes the Life Triumphant.

"The Life Triumphant is that which places what a man gives to the world in creative expression far ahead of that which he takes from it of the creations of others. And it should be every man's greatest ambition to be that kind of man. With that desire in the heart of every man there could be no greed or selfish unbalance, nor could there be exploitation of other men, or hatred, or war, or fear of war.

"The impregnation of that desire into a new age will be the makings of the next stage of his journey from the jungle of his beginnings to a full awareness of Light which awaits all mankind on the mountaintop of its journey's end."

Of such was Martha Mood made. Of such is her heritage.

GLENN TUCKER
art critic,
San Antonio Light

A few human beings in this world manage to climb to the top of the mountain. We know this not because they tell us that they have been to the summit, for most people who have made the ascent rarely, if ever, talk about it. Nor is it easy for anyone to misrepresent the truth in this particular area of life, because the proof of the experience usually manifests itself not only in one's countenance, but also in one's acts. If you looked into Martha Mood's eyes, you could see the reflections of the mountain peaks; if you experienced what she created, you know with certainty that she has scaled some of the highest and sheerest cliffs.

One of the distinct advantages of making it to the very top of the mountain is the opportunity it provides to examine an extraordinary view. Obviously, there is far more involved in the peek from the peak than a mere change in one letter of the alphabet, for what is actually involved is a glimpse of what Coleridge called the mighty alphabet of the universe. Like Loren Eiseley, Martha knew that "the very flight of birds is a writing to be read." What she observed from the summit was a monumental portrait of interrelation, of what we refer to in contemporary terms as the art of "putting it all together." She saw with compelling clarity how every extant entity is a part of the whole creation and how every individual unit is inexorably interlocked and, consequently, dependent upon every other unit. The illumination of this truth was so intense that it left an indelible tracery on the very core of Martha's being and became the cosmic map for her life's journey. She held every mineral, vegetable, insect, fish, reptile, bird, animal and man sacred, and she treated

160

them all with understanding, love and compassion. In summary, she was "Schweitzeresque!"

Perhaps the Golden Gate Bridge of her native San Francisco serves as an apt symbol for Martha Mood's life in the sense that Shelley implied in his poem, "The Cloud," when he wrote:

> *From cape to cape, with a bridge-like shape*
> *Over a torrent sea,*
> *Sunbeam-proof, I hand hang like a roof,—*
> *The mountains its columns be.*

Martha descended from the mountain top quite often, for she took seriously the wise suggestion of the ancient Arabic mystics, the Sufis, who aver that while it is necessary for man to withdraw from his daily routine to attempt spiritual purification through meditation, it is equally incumbent upon man to return to his regular life pattern and to apply the fruits of this contemplative period. Long ago, she had found the undiscovered truth, which we generally refer to as a secret, that poets and philosophers, not economists and politicians, really guide the world, for it is the artist's prerogative to indicate subtly the motivating forces and possible alternatives for man. Her own life pattern like that of many creative people was comprised of the usual academic training, the experiences of expert teaching, the accomplishments through numerous exhibitions and prizes, the success of being included in many distinguished private and public collections.

161

What was strikingly different about her life was her consistent ability to convert the inevitable bittersweet aspects of the human condition into precious banes. She knew how to refashion adversity into a polishing stone. Through a lifetime of artistic expression, she joined the rare band of human beings like the Psalmists, Schiller, Beethoven, Eiseley and Chardin, who created, each in his own inimitable way, hymns of praise to the universe. Hers came in a variety of media including photography, ceramics, sculpture and stitchery. It does not matter whether the aesthetic statement came in the form of light fixtures, fountains, sculptured murals or wall decorations, they are all pulsating with life, trembling with tenderness, vibrating with spirit!

Artists like Martha Mood have helped lay to rest once and for all the academic question about the innate potential of media as well as the divisive margin between craft and art. What person can be said to be an artist who is not an accomplished craftsman? What craftsman can be said to produce quality work who is not at heart a genuine artist endowed with intuition, imagination and emotion? True Mozartian that she was, Martha was quick to discover "hidden treasures" everywhere and reluctant to discard what to most would appear to be trivial and commonplace, devoid of beauty and value. She did not desire to possess things, for she knew full well that whatever we have we "borrow" for a very little while. To her, the smallest and seemingly most insignificant object was potentially beautiful, so she held it in the palm of her heart long enough to endow it with her own individual artistry and then release it again as

162

though she had found an injured bird, protected it while it recuperated and gave it back its freedom with renewed strength and sheen for all the world to share. Martha, who could reach down and pick up anything from a hunk of clay to a swatch of cloth and make it sing, showed us how utterly ridiculous and futile it is to waste time engaging in superficial controversy. In essence, what she did was to open herself up so as to become a clear vessel through which creativity could pour unhampered. As a result, she mastered the mystical art of converting soil into stardust!

Martha, the flowers of the earth, the spray of the sea and the winged of the air were all one! Truly, she was one of the very rare souls who did take a stitch in time, a stitch so lovely that it is quite possible that she helped to save the proverbial nine—planets as well as stitches—one of which might even be this very needy earth!

AMY FREEMAN LEE
artist, author, lecturer, and art critic,
with a particular involvement in the humane ethics movement
(from the program for The University of Texas Medical School
posthumous show of Mood's work, November, 1972)

VIII

THE PORTUGUESE TAPESTRIES

Portalegre, Portugal. *Photographs for this chapter by Al Weber.*

Tapestry is one of the glories of the art world. There is probably no other art form whose history is so interwoven with the fortunes of nations, their lore and literature. It is a brilliant medium and certainly one of the most prized. At the Grand Palais in Paris in the 1970s, the Metropolitan Museum of Art medieval tapestry exhibition was referred to as a dazzling display of "woolen jewels."

Tapestry weaving, which flourished for centuries in Europe, nearly died out in the twentieth century. Jean Lurçat and a group of his friends, still using traditional techniques, made a fresh start in France in the late 1930s. Today the revival continues, giving promise of an even more magnificent future. Interest in the acquisition of tapestries as examples of an historical art form, as precious family heirlooms, and as valuable investments is growing rapidly. The resurgence continues in important weaving centers: Aubusson and the Gobelins in France; Guy Fino's Manufactura de Tapeçarias de Portalegre in Portugal; workshops in Belgium, Poland, Yugoslavia, Czechoslavakia, Brazil, and other areas. Japan is one of the latest countries where the tapestry industry is reviving.

The present-day interest in tapestry no doubt has been stimulated by the development of modern architecture. The large expanses of bare walls in contemporary buildings offer an excellent setting for the warmth and splendor of the woven wall hangings, and often the interior of a home or commercial building is planned around the focal point of a magnificent tapestry.

The paintings of many contemporary artists have been translated into the tapestry medium and are available in the art marketplace. At Aubusson, hundreds of tapestries are woven annually from designs of famous artists—Louise Nevelson, Robert Motherwell, Frank Stella, Helen Frankenthaler, Alexander Calder, Jean Arp, Man Ray. There is renewed interest in this art form throughout Europe, and in the United States exhibits of medieval and modern tapestry in museums from New York to Los Angeles and San Francisco give continuing evidence of the tapestry revival. A variety of styles is developing with France's Sonia Delaunay and Brazil's Jean Gillon (geometrics), America's June Wayne and Sylvia Carewe and France's André Vilár (abstractions), Poland's Teresa Muszynska, Yugoslavia's Jagoda Buic and Spain's Josef Grau-Garriga (free form), Poland's Magdalena Abakonowicz (fiber sculpture), and others.

The Portuguese have been creating the designs of their own artists, João Tavares, Renato Torres, Jose de Almada Negreiros, C. Botelho, Maria Velez, Sá Nogueria, Charrua, Maria Flávia, Rogerio Ribeiro,

Guy Fino and Lester Kierstead Henderson.

Amandio Silva, Guilherme Camarinha, and Vieira De Silva, as well as foreign artists Jean Lurçat, Lars Gynning, Sidney Nolan, Arthur Boyd, Mathieu Mategot, and Danielle Moser.

But despite the vigor and the promise, the future of tapestry weaving is uncertain, according to Guy Fino, who has stated that "because of increased costs in Europe, it may not be possible to produce tapestries on a commercial level for very long. Tapestry woven by the individual artist, as in Yugoslavia and Czechoslavakia, may continue for many years, but weaving tapestries as we do in Portalegre, hand-crafted on looms, may not always be possible, due to economics."

This, in Fino's opinion, will escalate the value of tapestries even further, as new sources become more difficult to obtain.

Martha Mood is one of the few American artists whose work has been recreated in tapestry at the house of Fino. In 1972, when it became obvious that the artist was seriously ill, Lester Henderson talked to her about the possibility of having tapestries woven from her stitcheries. The Portuguese workshops were selected following an extensive investigation of weavers available and the decision that the Fino group could best capture the detail and spirit of the Mood work.

The little village of Portalegre, where for centuries the people have "worked the wool," is located in the hills of eastern Portugal. In the sixteenth century it was already an important location for the processing and weaving of woolen goods, as the official court supplier of mourning cloth on the occasion of the King's (Cardinal Dom Henrique's) death. Individual craftspeople in the city wove the black fabric for the royal family. There was no central workshop.

The town's importance as a cultural center was marked by one of the most outstanding schools of theology in the Iberian Peninsula, the Colégio de São Sebastião, run by Jesuits. During the time of the Marquis de Pombal, Prime Minister of King Joseph I (1771), the Jesuits were stamped out and the convent and college converted into one of the first woolen mills, Fábrica Real (Royal Factory), as part of the government's industrialization program.

A number of foreign technicians, including the Larcher brothers, were called in to initiate this mill. Joseph Larcher left the factory two

First a color transparency is made of an original stitchery and projected on graph paper to the required size. Here an artisan traces the design in detail.

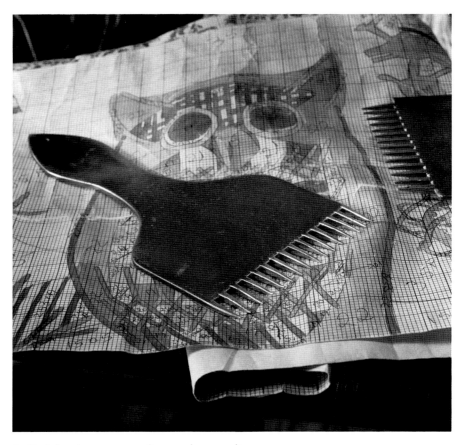
A finished pattern after color coding.

years later to start his own dyeing plant, doing commission work for the many wool craftsmen in the area. The Larcher plant later became the Fábrica de Lanifícios de Portalegre—today Francisco Fino, Lda., an internationally known textile plant established by the Fino family.

The Fino operation, exporting 70% of its output (in 1975), is one of the most up-to-date factories of its kind in the whole of Europe, producing textiles for men's clothing. In 1965, Francisco Fino, in association with Imperial Chemical Industries, set up another plant at Portalegre, Finicisa-Fibras Sintéticas, SARL, for the production of terylene polyester fibers, widening its scope.

Guy Fino is the head of the textile plant and the tapestry workshop. It was in 1946 that he and his family, with the Peixeiro family, became interested in promoting the revival of tapestry, playing an important role in its rebirth. While the textile plant had been established as a commercial enterprise, the tapestries are a labor of love for Fino, an outgrowth of his consuming interest in fine art as well as the family tradition of weaving.

Fino was born in Covilha, Portugal, the headquarters of the Portuguese wool textile industry. His father, Francisco De Sales Fernandes Fino, and grandfather, Manuel Fernandes Fino, had a small factory at the time the father was invited to reopen the Fábrica de Lanifícios—the only wool textile factory in Portalegre in 1929. The nine-year-old Guy went with his parents to Portalegre, returning to Covilha in 1932, where the father still maintained his factory.

In 1939, Francisco Fino was invited to become a partner in the Portalegre mill. His acceptance was the beginning of what was to be a significant milestone in the history of tapestry weaving. Prior to 1947, when the tapestry weaving was begun, production had been exclusively textiles. Starting with a workshop in the former Fábrica Real, the Finos developed a plant for making handwoven wall tapestries which soon became known the world over and which have since won many awards.

In 1952 the French Embassy organized a huge tapestry exhibition in the Fine Arts Museum in Lisbon, showing tapestries from the Middle Ages to that time. Simultaneously, Fino organized an exhibition in the National Secretariat for Information (SNI) and displayed two of his large

Selecting yarns and recording color code numbers on patterns.

tapestries woven from cartoons of Portuguese painter Guilherme Camarinha and purchased by the government for the Palace of the Governor of Madeira Islands in Funchal. The technicians from the French group, invited to see the exhibit, termed it "magnificent," and this was the debut of a new technique in the tapestry art.

Today only a part of the former Royal Factory is used for tapestry weaving, with some areas leased out and others unused. A museum in the building exhibits tapestries signed by some of the world's greatest artists in this field. In 1975 eighty weavers were producing more

Weaving from the back on vertical loom (or frame) developed
in Portalegre. The technique permits the reproduction of
full-size tapestries up to 44 yards long and of unlimited height
in a single piece.

tapestries than any other single facility under one roof in the world,
with 80% of the production being exported.

While weavers such as the Gobelins reproduce tapestries of
historical designs, Fino concentrates on the best of the contemporary
artists, in the belief that it is incumbent upon today's weavers to
immortalize the art of their time, as the artisans of centuries past
did theirs.

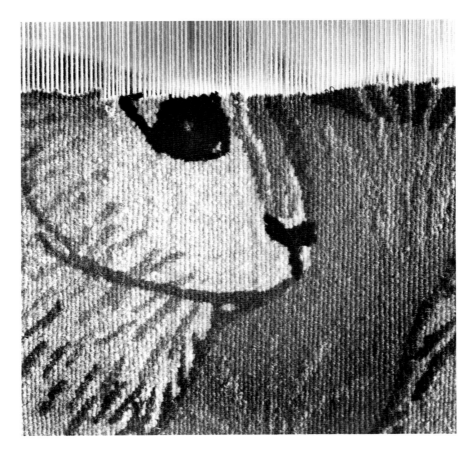

Partially woven Mood tapestry.

Drawing upon his heritage, Guy Fino has brought the ancient art and new technology together—a synthesis that has become known as the modern Portuguese school. The Portuguese technique consists of involving the warp by the decorative weft and weaving from one selvage to the other. Weaving is done on vertical looms, or frames. While the Gobelins also use vertical looms, theirs are of a completely different design, with a beam for the warp and a beam for rolling the tapestry. Fino also uses this system but with small section warp beams instead of a single beam, and the woven tapestry is not rolled on a beam.

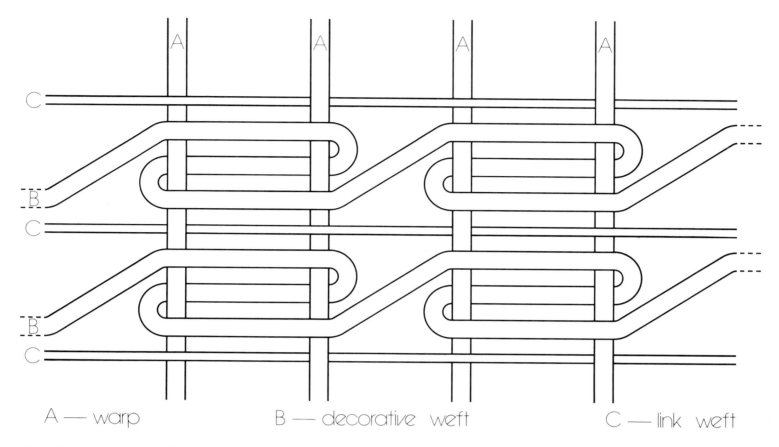

A — warp   B — decorative weft   C — link weft

The Fino continuous loop stitch ensures tightness of the weave. Note additional
weft yarn between each row of stitches, for additional strength.

The purpose of the vertical frame, in addition to permitting the
reproduction of large tapestries in one piece, is to maintain the warp
stretched in order for weavers to use the horizontal decorative weft,
which is wool yarn.

A continuous loop stitch is used, with an additional shot of fine
link weft in plain weave between each row of stitches, in order to avoid
later sewing together of adjacent vertical color areas. The system
encompasses 161 stitches per square inch, a staggering figure when
one considers that this adds up to 205,032 stitches per square yard.

Fino's weaving lines in Portugal.

Taking into account the fact that each stitch can be divided to obtain small details, the figure mounts up impressively. Each weaver completes approximately one square yard per month.

Wool is carefully selected; carding, spinning, and dyeing are done in the Fino yarn mill, following which the yarns are twisted to the required resistance and strength. Because of the facilities required to produce suitings in the Fino textile plant, the widest range of colors is available, produced from fine dyes demanded to withstand exposure to the strong sunlight of the Mediterranean countries. If a required color is not among the vast stores, the dyeing plant can create the specific color requested. Thousands of shades are classified in a data processing system—a key part of the high quality production process and the incredible faithfulness of the color translations of the Mood stitcheries. The eight-strand decorative weft yarn offers numerous possibilities for color mixtures and gradations.

Although the Fino plant does not produce its own cotton yarn, it buys the best possible quality in a single yarn and twists it to obtain a fine warp. In this technique the tapestry is hung from and supported by the warp thread—the stronger part. In the traditional technique, weaving is done in the horizontal position and the tapestry usually turned 90 degrees to hang it. The part that supports the weight is the decorative weft—the weaker part. Not critical in a small tapestry, the weight becomes significant in a weaving of more than two yards.

The Fino method of translating the design into the tapestry took some years of experimentation. In the old method, the weaver approximated the color and design by eye. Other methods of copying the work through mechanical means resulted in faithful reproduction, but damaged the original art work so that it could not be used again for optimum results.

The Portalegre workshop uses the traditional method of collaboration between an artist designing a cartoon (or painting) and a weaver executing it, with the original reproduced according to the artist's directions. Normally, a cartoon must be painted to the same size as the eventual tapestry. If a tapestry is to vary in size from the original art, a cartoon must be produced to the tapestry size—a time-consuming process. At Fino's, even small-scale art may be used. The original art is photographed. The resulting transparency is projected on graph paper with each square being the exact size of each stitch, or point. An artisan traces the pattern with pencil, and then paints in the design with watercolors. The colored yarns are selected by matching them to the original stitchery and recording the code numbers on the graph (stencil).

The Portalegre tapestries, woven to last six hundred years, with proper care will undoubtedly even exceed this life expectancy and become cherished heirlooms to be handed down for many generations as among the finest of their time.

The Mood tapestries are larger than the original stitcheries because in the tapestry the yarn threads are all of one size (five threads per CM), while in the stitchery some of the cloth used has much finer threads. It requires a given number of threads to weave a particular part of the design, and it will take the same number of threads to make the same design with the thicker weaving yarn. The designers thus must

Another view of the former Royal Factory, now the tapestry workshops.

determine the size increase, which is dependent on the ratio of thread sizes of key parts of the design.

A number of Mood designs have been woven, in limited quantities. The Mood stitcheries lend themselves ideally to the weaving medium, and lose none of their richness, although they were not designed with tapestries in mind and are a separate and distinct art form. The Fino–Mood tapestries are in a class by themselves. In the Moods, one perceives a three-dimensional effect not to be found in most traditionally woven tapestries. This is not only because of the artist's creation of depth in her stitchery designs, but because the tapestries depict what was initially an actual fabric design. In contrast, the creations of some contemporary artists, while brilliant as paintings, fall short as tapestries, suggesting that from the outset the artist was thinking in terms of a canvas instead of a loom.

The Fino techniques in weaving and color coding have resulted in great accuracy and vibrancy in the final translation of the Mood stitcheries, which are considered to be among the finest of Fino's productions, and are receiving as much acclaim as did the original stitcheries. The particular affinity between the work of Martha Mood and the Fino art of tapestry has brought about a sort of artistic alchemy—resulting in a new, exciting art expression that is attracting attention from some of the most knowledgeable people in the art world.

EPILOGUE

Martha Mood did so many good deeds and was always casting good thoughts for so many people that it flowed back to her. I feel that her being one with the universe gave her that perpetual energy through which she was able to produce this continuous stream of wonderful art.

I knew in the moment I met Martha and looked into those big brown eyes that something very special had touched my life. I could feel the emanations from her and I still feel them. It's amazing, in my own work when I hit a stumbling block now, I can close my eyes and it's as if Martha is there saying, "Push the clay up a little here. Lift this line. Or make this a little longer. Change the eye, the expression."

It's almost as if her energy is in the universe—it's for people to pick up when they know her and know her work. Like dropping a rock into a pond and the waves keep going out. If you tune in with them, they're still there.

I want so much for young artists and more people to be allowed to know her work and to know her. I want people to know that such a person has existed . . . and that she is still here.

JULIA BLACK

COMMENTARY

Like everyone else, I fell in love with her. Her eyes were so beautiful, as was everything about her. Although she had had an automobile accident which had scarred her face, it was still the face of an eager child.

I don't recall discussing theology, church or the Bible with Martha, but she was more innately religious than some of the people who talk a lot about God. Her stitcheries, to me, are as much an expression of love and a celebration of life as were St. Francis' verses in praise of Brother Sun, Sister Moon and the stars, Brother Fire and Sister Water, and "divers fruits and coloured flowers." She was a Franciscan Fioretti, in her joyous spirit, in her disregard of money. Monk's cloth and gunnysack formed the background for most of her work, and no leftover scrap from her own or a neighbor's sewing basket was too insignificant for use in a face, a flower or a bird's wing. She made new creations of humble and castoff materials as surely as St. Francis' embrace transformed lepers and outcasts into new beings.

In the Portuguese tapestry which currently hangs in the entry room of the New Harmony Inn, one finds her own accurate interpretation of St. Francis in a woodland setting. The punch line, for me, lies not in the docile animals at his feet, or in the white birds of purity and goodness about the head, but in the dark, redeemed bird which he holds tenderly near his heart.

In the early days of our friendship, I remember giving Martha a lecture about charging more for her creations. "Now Martha," I scolded, "you have a family. You're a woman of great talent, genius, in fact, and you mustn't undersell yourself." She was about to have a show in Dallas. "Raise your prices to at least $500," I said.

She returned from Dallas laughing her head off. Winthrop Rockefeller had bought a hanging for $500. I said, "I don't think he would have touched it for any less." That same stitchery would sell for many thousands today if it were available.

I think the muses cease to visit a true artist when he or she becomes interested solely in what they are getting. That is why Martha's output, her creative flow, never froze. That's why Rembrandt died broke.

She could not bear pretense; she could see through to the core of people, immediately knew their motives. She had an intuition about that, a deep intuition.

When a great genius comes upon the scene and one hears him, as when I heard Gustav Mahler's First Symphony, I remarked to a friend: "He has heard what no man has heard before." That's the mark of genius. When you see a Martha Mood, you realize that she's seen what no one has seen before. This is what separates genius from talent.

JANE OWEN
art sponsor implementing a renewal movement
in the historic town of New Harmony, Indiana,
as a spiritual, cultural, and art center

INDEX OF ILLUSTRATIONS

ACKNOWLEDGMENTS

Kathleen Devlin, special editing; Sylvia Lovell-Cooper and Ann Forman, technical consulting; Al Weber and Ulric Meisel, technical and photographic assistance; Anne R. P. Henderson and Sandy Rosen, critique; Sydney Demarest, copyright and proofreading; Shirlie Stoddard, proofreading; Cathleen Vigneaux, photographic assistant; Mary D'Eau Claire, Peggy Land, and Tina Panziera, illustration cataloguing.

Acknowledgment is made to the following publishers and copyright holders for permission to use their material in The Sublime Heritage of Martha Mood.

Excerpts from an article by Elise Jerram from *The Sunday Peninsula Herald,* Peninsula Life Section, July 13, 1975. Copyright © 1975 by The Monterey Peninsula Herald Company.

Excerpts from an article by Martha Mood from *House Beautiful,* October, 1962. Copyright © 1962 by The Hearst Corporation.

The Sublime Heritage of Martha Mood *had many authors—Martha's family, friends, associates and students; members of the art and design world; and those who felt her impact only in passing. To them, whose words have created this book, our gratitude.*

Mr. Morley Baer; Mrs. Julia Black; Mrs. Susan Bragstad; Mr. and Mrs. Charles Brown; Mrs. Ruth Buol; Miss Jean Cauthorn; Mrs. Enid Collins; Mrs. Lessi Ellen Culmer; Helen and Walter Del Tredici; Mrs. Ann Drought; Mr. and Mrs. O'Neil Ford; Miss Martha Fuller; Mrs. Marjorie Guillory; Margaret and Benjamin Hammond; Mrs. Jake Hershey; Mrs. Mildred Horne; Mrs. Toria Hubbard; Reverend Raymond Judd, Jr., Trinity University, San Antonio, Texas; Mr. Robert L. Kidd; Mary and Michael Lance; Dolores and Felipe Latorre; Mrs. Amy Freeman Lee; Mr. Edgar Lehmann; Mrs. Caroline Maessen; Mrs. Barbara M. Meyer; Mr. Richard E. Miller; Mrs. Louise Mann Millikan; Mr. Beaumont Mood; Mrs. Winnie Noah; Mrs. Jane Owen; Mrs. Margaret B. Pace; Mrs. Martha Parrish; Mr. Roger Rasbach; Mr. John R. Rouse, the Wichita Art Museum; Mrs. Ramona Seeligson; Mrs. Glenna Simmons; Mrs. Virginia Smith; Margaret and Billy Steele; Mr. Glenn Tucker, San Antonio Light; Dorothy and August Wagele; Mrs. John H. Webb, Jr.; Mr. Robert A. Weinstein; Mrs. Glasfira Williams; Mr. Robert K. Winn; Mrs. Ann Woodward.

Our thanks to the following owners of Martha Mood stitcheries which appear in this book.

Mr. and Mrs. Jack R. Ambler; Mr. and Mrs. Gordon T. Beaham, III; Mr. and Mrs. Ronald E. Chamness; Mr. Edward D. Cobb; Mr. Trammell Crow; Mrs. James M. Crump; Dr. and Mrs. George Ehni; Mr. and Mrs. H. R. Galloway; Dr. and Mrs. Alan D. Harley; Mr. George F. Jewett, Jr.; The John M. Kings; Mrs. Steinman Nunan; Mrs. Doris H. Vickers.

The balance of the stitcheries pictured are from the collection of Lester Kierstead Henderson.

Joseph Stacey

Editor of *Arizona Highways* magazine from 1970 through 1975, Joseph Stacey produced the distinguished 1974-1975 "Collector Series" of Indian Arts and Crafts of the Southwest for the publication. He is presently a writer, lecturer, and consultant to publishers and corporate art collectors.

Lester Kierstead Henderson

An art collector and agent, Lester Henderson has been responsible for the rise in fame of numerous artists, including Martha Mood. For many years he has also been a leading family portrait photographer, numbering many famous citizens among his clients.

Shirley Koploy

Shirley Koploy is a journalist and short story writer. Her credits include articles for *SourceBook* magazine; *LIFE in California; Ms.* magazine; *Beverly Hills* magazine; a short story, "Boat Ride," for the literary magazine, *Line;* numerous freelance articles for consumer and trade publications.

Display type in Delphian Open and Optima; text type in Zapf Book Light and Zapf Book Light Italic. Composition by Graphic Typesetting Service, Los Angeles. Lithographed by George Rice & Sons under the supervision of Andrew G. Murray. Bound by Hiller Industries, Salt Lake City, Utah. Printed on Mead Paper, Dayton, Ohio, made especially for this book. Endpapers in Strathmore Beau Brilliant Seabright Blue. Design and layout by Wendy Cunkle Calmenson.

Volume I: Limited Commemorative Edition, biography of Martha Mood, with 32 full-color reproductions, 27 black and white photographs, 208 pages.

Volume II: Limited Commemorative Edition, more than 100 full-color reproductions, with limited text, approximately 200 pages.